How to use your
job:
Core
Skills and Employability

by Rachel Sumner

British library cataloguing-in-publication data
A catalogue record for this book is available from the British Library.
Published by:
Kaplan Publishing UK
Unit 2 The Business Centre
Molly Millars Lane
Wokingham
Berkshire
RG41 2QZ

ISBN 978-0-85732-486-3

First edition published 2012

Printed and bound in Great Britain.

CONTENTS

ACKNOWLEDGEMENTS

We are extremely grateful to the individuals and organisations whose quotations appear within this book. These contributors and, where relevant, their organisations, are acknowledged throughout the book wherever their quotations appear.

CHAPTER 1

Introduction/Context

Employability Overload!!

According to CEOs, such as Sam Laidlaw of Centrica plc, it has never been more important to develop and demonstrate employability skills. Given the competition in the graduate labour market and the increasing pressure on business to recruit 'talent', candidates who can provide evidence of these skills and a clear indication of their intention to develop these skills yet further will be best placed to secure employment.

In May of 2011 it was reported in an article by TARGETjobs that more than 70% of employers interviewed believed that graduates should do more to develop their employability skills as these were regarded more highly than degree subject or result to graduate recruiters.

No matter where we look in the media currently the topic of graduate employability seems to be high on everyone's agenda. Graduates bemoaning the fact that they cannot find jobs having spent three to four years and thousands of pounds on their studies, employers complaining that the graduates they do recruit are unable to do the jobs they were recruited for or alternatively they cannot find graduates whom they want to recruit in the first place and government spokespeople warning of a looming skills crisis which will hamper the economic recovery. It seems that "employability" has become a core skill, a fundamental component of everyone's "tool-kit".

Whichever way you look at it there seems to be a veritable 'overload' of concern about the employability (or lack of employability!!) of graduates. As an undergraduate or recent graduate yourself it is likely that you are feeling the pressure to 'find a job' once your degree studies are complete and given this media frenzy around the topic I suspect that the pressure is increasing.

Therefore, let me share with you why this book is a MUST BUY:

- it seeks to share more of the **reality** of the situation around graduate employability
- it will assist you in **demonstrating** your employability to prospective or current employers and
- it will enable you to **use the skills** you acquired during your degree (and possibly from previous work experience) to greater advantage in the workplace.

In the latter part of this first chapter entitled 'How to Use This Book' I will explain how together we are going to achieve this.

> “The market is tough so try & build your skills up through extra-curricular activities”
>
> Freelance Students (via Twitter) www.freelancestudents.co.uk

A Matter of Perspective...

Before we go any further together, let's be clear about the perspective that has been taken in this book regarding graduate employability so that you can be sure that this book is worth your 'hard-earned' money!!

Firstly, there are a number of assumptions made by the author of this book.

Assumption No.1

You chose to take the degree you are currently (or have been recently) studying for to find a job (work) in a related field on the completion of your studies.

Assumption No.2

You are currently studying (or have studied recently) for a full degree (or professional qualification).

Assumption No.3

You are keen to **maximise** the 'return on your investment' of the time and money you have spent on your studies.

Assumption No.4

In order to maximize the 'return on your investment' you are willing to spend a little further **time and effort** to read this book and undertake the activities therein.

Assumption No.5

You recognize that your employability is not only affected by the knowledge and skills you possess, but also by more 'tricky' issues such as **personality** and **attitude**.

It is equally important that we are clear about what this book alone CANNOT do for you. It cannot:

- guarantee you a job/find you work
- train you in all the necessary skills in which you may be lacking
- magically resolve any issues that were inherent in your programme of study
- address any of those 'tricky' issues, such as attitude (although given that you have recognised the value of working on your employability by buying this book it does suggest you have something of the right attitude!!).

" Employers don't give jobs to work experience and education. They give them to you. "

Barry Crawford, Frank HR (via Twitter) www.frank-hr.com

Background

The reason why it is so important that we are clear about the perspective taken within this book is so that you recognise the fact that the design of degrees and professional qualifications has moved inconsistently (between institutions, across sectors and educational philosophies) towards the development of graduate employability through their programmes of study (the modules/courses involved).

There are some who would argue that studying for a degree should have nothing to do with finding employment upon graduation but purely be the study of a subject about which we are individually curious for the sake of knowledge acquisition alone. There is a very small part of me that can see real merit in this perspective, but we live in a reality of economic need where only a tiny percentage of our global population have sufficient financial means to choose to study simply for pleasure. For the vast majority it is considered the route to greater economic well-being through the acquisition not only of knowledge but also of a range of skills that enable the successful graduate to achieve employment in a workplace which demands that knowledge and those skills.

And here is where we hit THE SNAG that seems to be consuming so many column inches, sound bites and tags. CAN we (students/graduates/employers/joe public etc) safely assume that:

- those that design degrees and professional qualifications **know** the knowledge and skills that the workplace is looking for?
- degrees and professional qualifications are able to 'produce' graduates who **possess** that knowledge and those skills?
- degree and professional qualifications are sufficiently flexible and responsive to adapt to the **changing needs** of the workplace in a **timely** fashion?

And I am afraid the answer is 'No!'...or maybe 'Not entirely.' As mentioned earlier, there is still significant inconsistency in the way that differing institutions and sectors are addressing these issues and as a result graduates of different degree programmes, even within the same institution, may find they have not been 'equally' prepared for the workplace.

As a result of this it is impossible to write a book that will perfectly match everyone's degree or professional qualification exactly, but there is some hope for us all. A number of the key educational and governmental stakeholders, in consultation with a range of businesses, have made real progress in recent months in defining the KEY employability skills[1], many of which had previously been recognised by agencies such as the UK's QCA[2] as a fundamental requirement of many UK degrees and professional qualifications and therefore included (in a wide variety of ways – some more successful than others!) in the relevant programmes of study. There is therefore some hope that within your UK degree or professional qualification you will, at some point, have covered some (or all) of the employability skills covered in this book.

And if not, by reading this book, exploring the micro-site (www.kaplanpublishing.co.uk/coreskills), undertaking the activities and taking advantage of the useful links and further reading suggested you will be able to address your own 'skills gap' in preparation for your entry into the workplace or to improve the way in which you are currently demonstrating your value to your existing employer.

1 See Appendix

2 Qualifications and Curriculum Authority

THOSE Employability Skills

So what are the skills that the workplace is seemingly demanding that graduates possess? A review of the most recent research and publications in this area suggest the following skill categories:

- self-management
- teamworking
- business and customer awareness
- problem solving
- communication and literacy
- application of numeracy
- application of information technology
- entrepreneurialism.

Needless to say, in a text of this size it would be impossible to cover all the skills required within each of these categories so we have identified a range of the key skills within each, which make up the following chapters, but in the back of the book you'll find a list of **all** the skills identified in the research for your information.

So, as promised earlier, let's take a look at how the book is going to help you in improving your employability.

Employability skills may have been taught as part of your formal programme of study or alternatively been part of a supplementary programme of mandatory or optional activities.

Equally employability skills may or may not have been assessed as part of your programme of study, possibly you simply received some informal feedback on your skills or maybe not even that.

Whatever experience you have had of 'employability skills development', the key method used by this book in enhancing your employability is by giving you the opportunity, via a range of tools, to reflect on and learn from the experience you had of using these skills (either during your programme of study and/or through previous work experience) and then to plan for and/or actually try out what you have learned.

This method is an adaptation of Kolb's Experiential Learning Cycle theory[3] in which Kolb expands on the work of Kurt Lewin (a renowned modern psychologist) by developing a theory of adult learning which can begin at any stage in the cycle and continue cyclically as a continually 'renewing' learning process.

Given the changing nature of the skills in demand in the workplace this is therefore an appropriate method to utilise as you will be required throughout your career to continually improve your skills. Kolb himself is an educational theorist who has a particular interest in executive and professional education.

The method is broken down into a number of steps in each chapter of the book.

- Review
- Assess
- Apply
- Reflect
- Evaluate
- Checklist

Step 1

Review (outline recognised good practice in the skill)

In this step we undertake a short review of some of the key theories and concepts related to the skill in question – just to make sure you haven't missed anything fundamental!

You'll also find some useful links and suggested reading here to other helpful sources that cover the theory and concepts in more detail.

Now would also be the time to dig out any notes, previous materials, feedback (formal or otherwise) you've acquired on this particular skill.

3 Kolb D.A. (1984) 'Experiential Learning experience as a source of learning and development', New Jersey: Prentice Hall

Step 2

Assess (strengths/weaknesses: include diagnostic tool)

Now comes the potentially 'tough bit' where you are expected to undertake an honest assessment of your own strengths and weaknesses in this area.

Don't panic – no one else is going to see your answers!

Equally, you won't necessarily be flying 'solo' here. You can draw on any of the formal or informal feedback you've previously received or even seek out new feedback from current peers, managers or direct reports.

REMEMBER - The more honest your assessment here the more value you will gain from this whole process.

Step 3

Application (how might skill be applied)

During your programme of study your employability skills development may have happened through some particularly 'contrived' activities which didn't feel much like the real world. However, you are now expected to be able to apply these skills in the realities of the modern workplace.

In this section we look at ways in which the skill is really going to be applied and consider some of the common challenges so that you can see them coming!

Step 4

Reflect (what have I learned?)

So far you have reviewed, assessed and considered the application of the skill in the workplace; all quite 'active' steps which required you largely to 'do stuff'. Now comes the 'thinking part' where you make sense of what you've learnt from the previous steps.

This may be obvious with some skills but with other skills the learning may be more subtle and nuanced and therefore more difficult to 'spot'.

This is however a critical step in the process and is often the one missed or overlooked during your studies as you rush headlong from one assessment to the next, focusing on the grade or mark and not really having the time (or maybe the opportunity) to make sense of the feedback[4].

Reflection goes beyond just gaining knowledge to:

- exploring the foundations of that knowledge
- strengthening understanding, and
- increasing awareness of the values and attitudes that influence it.

The process of reflection typically has three stages:

- returning to experience - a detailed recounting or recollection of the events
- attending to the feelings, both positive and negative, that have been prompted by the experience
- re-evaluating that experience in the light of these stages and the learner's intent, and self-knowledge, bringing in new knowledge that has been gained through the process.

NOW is the time to make sense of your learning.

4 The whole 'feedback' issue is hugely contentious in itself given the criticism of the inconsistent quality and quantity of feedback given in many institutions.

Step 5

Evaluate (reach a judgement on personal performance)

So the time has come. How do you judge/rate/score yourself in this skill set?

Recognising that this is a largely personal judgement and that we all have tendencies to either overstate or underplay our own performance, once again the greatest value in this step will come from an HONEST judgement of your own skill.

Step 6

Checklist (what next...future development)

10/10 or 30%? However you've scored there needs to be a plan in place. Either to address the areas for improvement or to creatively find ways to make those top skills really work for you (and your employer!).

We take some time in this step to create a measurable plan of action to ensure all those key skills that are needed in your workplace are where you score highest.

Although we stated very clearly earlier that this book cannot guarantee you a job (or work) in your preferred field at the end of it, what it does seek to do is to assist you in developing a self-marketing strategy which really communicates these skills to a prospective or future employer. It's no good having all these great skills if:

- you don't tell anybody about them!
- you don't show them off at every and any appropriate opportunity!

So the final section of each chapter is dedicated to a range of self-marketing tips from professionals in the fields of recruitment and graduate talent management on how best to sell these critical **skills** during the selection process or better still 'on the job'!

Each chapter will contain a number of different tips many of which could work for a whole range of skills so are not necessarily for use with that skill only.

So in conclusion...

You have worked so hard to achieve all that you have done so far: getting a place on the degree course or professional qualification, spending hours poring over textbooks or your virtual learning environment, writing endless exams and pieces of coursework and generally spending several years of your life to achieve your career aspirations. Don't waste it all now by not taking every opportunity to make yourself as employable as you possibly can.

> *"Take advantage of everything offered and use the time to discover what you like."*
>
> Mona Chegui (via Twitter), Human Resources Officer, www.msc.org

Self-Marketing Tips

Using the table below, carry out a quick personal assessment of your skills in each of these areas. Don't worry if you don't know, at this stage, exactly what each covers because that's part of the purpose of this book…to ensure you do know and can develop and market these skills.

Score yourself using a points score between 0 and 10 where 0 = No skills in this area and 10 = Highly skilled in this area. Once again, be as honest as possible!

Cognitive Skills

Score ....

Problem Solving and Decision Making

Score ....

Research and Investigative Skills/Business Awareness

Score ....

IT

Score ....

Numeracy and Quantitative Skills

Score ....

Communication Skills

Score ....

Interpersonal Skills

Score ....

Teamworking Skills

Score ....

Self-Marketing Tips

Personal/Self-Management Skills

Score: ....

Stress Management Skills

Score: ....

Conflict Management Skills

Score: ....

Learning Skills

Score: ....

Self-Awareness

Score: ....

Emotional Intelligence

Score: ....

Skills for Entrepreneurship and Consultancy

Score: ....

CHAPTER 2

Business Awareness

Step 1

Review

Business awareness or commercial sensitivity is a specific skill set that is developed and honed over time. It is also somewhat market, sector or industry specific but there are some general skills that you can develop and demonstrate to any potential employer that will provide them with confidence that you have the ability to attune yourself to their organisation.

> *"Keep an open mind, employers crave real-life experience, look at the small firms, they can give really exciting opportunities."*
>
> Rob Coates, HR123 (via Twitter) www.hr123.co.uk

What is Business Awareness?

Business (or commercial) awareness could be defined as an interest in business and an understanding of the wider environment in which an organisation operates: its customers, competitors and suppliers.

It may also include an understanding of business economics and an appreciation of the business benefits and commercial realities from both the organisation's and the customer's perspectives.

Typically it includes awareness of the need for efficiency, cost-effectiveness, customer care and knowledge of the marketplace in which the business operates.

According to a 2009 survey by the CBI and UUK it is a major criterion for selecting candidates. The same survey found that 35% of employers were dissatisfied with the business and customer awareness of graduates.

Why is Business Awareness Important?

As stated above, employers are increasingly looking for applicants who can demonstrate business awareness and this is not only true of jobs in 'business' but even applicants for public sector positions need to demonstrate their commercial awareness as the public sector is under increasing pressure to demonstrate its financial efficiency and to compete with private firms.

If an applicant demonstrates a real awareness of the current challenges and opportunities facing the business it shows a number of things to the recruiter:

- research skills: the applicant clearly has skills related to information gathering and analysis
- knowledge: the applicant has at least a basic knowledge of the key drivers and factors that affect the business
- motivation: if an applicant has taken the time to undertake some research and develop a body of knowledge about the business there is evidently real motivation to secure the position
- make a contribution: applicants who have developed their business awareness are more likely to make a faster personal contribution to the success of the business than those who need time and support to do so....whom would you employ?

Developing Business Awareness

As suggested in the chapter introduction, developing your business awareness is an ongoing activity. If you develop some regular habits in this regard you'll probably be surprised how quickly your skills and knowledge develop. Also take advantage of colleagues, friends and family who are 'business aware'; quiz them about the current economic climate and the market or industry in which you're interested. People who like this kind of stuff tend to REALLY LIKE this stuff and are often more than happy to share their interest.

There are other other ways in which you can develop your business awareness.

1. Read the company's brochure and check their website for background information - don't just look at the "careers" section but also at the sections for clients, potential clients and staff.

2. Review their annual report – these are typically now available via the company's website or if not via your local business library (most major cities have one of these if your university doesn't).

3. Find out who the company's competitors are: you may well be asked this and to which ones you have applied! In some markets there is fierce competition between rival businesses and they have what is known as a 'gentleman's agreement' not to steal each other's staff even after they have left the business for a certain number of years – the intellectual property they hold is highly valuable and of a competitive nature. Also try to find out the size of the workforce, the turnover and profits of the company, its share price and key activities which interest you (this information can typically be found on the company website or in the annual report – 1. and 2. above).

4. Read the business press - the business pages of the major broadsheet newspapers should cover most of the background that you need, but the Financial Times and the Economist will be essential if you are applying for an analytical role. Of course these are all available online and will certainly be held in your local university or public library so this need not cost anything.

5. During your reading, look out for stories that will affect the organisation to which you are applying, or its clients, directly or indirectly. Current issues could include the recession, global debt, climate change and governance issues.

6. The relevant professional press such as Accountancy Age, Campaign, The Lawyer and others will keep you up-to-date with developments in the relevant sector.

7. Also try to catch business-related programmes on TV and radio such as Working Lunch, the Money Programme and World Business Review. 'Lighter' programmes such as Dragons' Den and The Apprentice also raise a number of business issues and can offer good material for discussion. If you can't view them on the day most are available via iPlayer (or equivalent) or podcasts that you can view or listen to in a spare moment.

<<

8. Relate your own experience to business. You may be doing part-time bar or retail work purely to earn money but this can also be used to gain an insight into business. What are the good and bad points about your employer? What is its target market? Who are its main competitors? How would you improve the company's image or profitability? Keep this in mind for Step 2.

If all this sounds like a lot of work please bear in mind the current 'condition' of the graduate labour market and remember how crucial it is that you set yourself apart from the hundreds, if not thousands, of other applicants for the role. It has been said many times that applying for a job is a job in itself! Try and treat it that way.

> *"Working is great experience. Even if it is not in your chosen field, it gives you valuable experience. Plus it allows you to meet people who are already working. Use them – network, ask questions, and especially find out what they do a daily basis. This will give you a better idea of different roles, and so help you apply for jobs in a systematic manner when the time comes."*
>
> Mona Chergui, Human Resources Officer, www.msc.org

Step 2

Assess

So it's time to assess your business awareness and consider an approach to researching a business of your choice, which may help you when the time comes to apply for a position.

Using either the company you had in mind when considering bullet point 8 in "Developing Business Awareness" above, or any other company you'd like to research, complete the table below as if you were preparing to apply for a position with them.

>>

Business research

Name and postal address of business (check the spelling)	
Website address: main	
Website address: graduate recruitment	
Outline of main business	What products does it make? What services does it provide? What is the organisation's mission statement? How can I explain what the business does in my own words?
Clients and customers	Who uses this organisation's products/ services? In which countries does this organisation operate?
Main competitors	What other organisations operate in this area or offer similar products/ services? How do these organisations compare?
Where is Head Office?	
Annual turnover/gross profit	
Recent news	Look at recent press releases and review a quality daily newspaper or its website – what are the important stories and headlines for this organisation?
Business values	What are its stated or implied core values?
What does the employer's brand say to me?	How does the organisation brand itself? What do I think about this?

<<

What are its policies relating to flexible working, equal opportunities (or other relevant issues)…?	
Awards	Has this organisation won any awards related to recruitment and workplace (e.g. TARGETjobs National Graduate Recruitment Awards, Best Employer Awards…) or its products and services?
What do current graduates say? (read profiles on the employer's website and at sites such as **TARGETjobs.co.uk**)	
Will I be based in one location or expected to travel to different offices and sites?	If mobility is required, when and how often will I be travelling and will this be international or within the UK?

Step 3

Application (how might skill be applied)

Writing recently about the social media advertising industry, TBG Digital CEO Simon Mansell listed a high level of commercial awareness as being amongst the key criteria when selecting new recruits into his business. He makes reference to the 2011 Apprentice winner, Tom Pellereau, who, although not exactly successful in the tasks set by Lord Sugar, remained in the running as a result of his commercial awareness and ability to think 'outside the box'. Mansell goes further by making the argument that by developing a deep understanding of their market and that of their clients TBG has been able to thrive in a fiercely competitive environment.

Similarly, property company Savills when recently interviewed by TARGETjobs described commercial awareness as being 'crucial' in the graduates that they employ.

>>

<<

In an ever-changing, global world, commercial or business awareness may well assist you in securing a position but it may well also be what keeps you in a position. In the current labour market where employers are faced with no shortage of applicants in many areas, human resource becomes more expendable and therefore employees are easier to replace with someone else who may well be more 'up to date' with current market conditions.

The challenge then is not only to develop your business awareness in preparation for applying for roles but also to develop the skills to maintain and enhance your awareness; to develop a professional 'radar' that enables you to capture all relevant information and then a system that enables you to analyse the information ready for application.

Consider

1. Maintaining a set of notes on related issues.
2. Developing a number of key contacts who can keep you abreast of market conditions.
3. Building an 'archive' of useful articles.
4. Using technology to keep you attuned to news, such as email alerts and RSS feeds.

Reflect (what have I learned?)

STOP!

By now you are likely to have gained a considerable amount of information about business awareness and possibly a sense of your own level of awareness. Hopefully, the exercise in Step 2 will have alerted you to any gaps in your skills and knowledge related to developing your business awareness.

However, let's just take some time to consider what you have learnt so far.

Task 1

Looking back on the business research exercise you undertook in Step 2, answer the following questions:

How did you find the research exercise itself? Did you know where and how to research this type of information?

What information was most difficult to find?

What information was most difficult to read/understand/access?

<<

How does this differ from research activities you've undertaken in the past?

Would you now feel sufficiently informed to apply for a position with the company you researched? If not, what further information would you require?

Task 2

Looking back on this and other experiences where you've had to demonstrate your business awareness, how do you feel about your level of awareness?

>>

Task 3

Re-read your answers to Tasks 1 and 2 above. Does anything you've written surprise you?

Now you've nearly reached the end of this chapter, what do you think you've learnt about business awareness and your own level of awareness?

If you are finding this difficult, imagine that you are commenting on someone else's answers to the Task 1 and 2 questions. What would you advise them about developing their business awareness?

Step 5

Evaluate (reach a judgement on personal performance)

So the time has come. How do you judge/rate/score your level of business awareness? Use the information from this chapter and the previous steps to inform your decision.

Score yourself using a scale of 0 – 10 where 0 = No Skills and 10 = Highly Skilled.

Score:

Return to the Self-Assessment you undertook at the end of Chapter 1 and note the score you gave yourself then for business awareness.

Self-Assessment Score:

Step 6

Check List (what next...future development)

Skill: Business Awareness

Area for Improvement	I need to.....	Sources of Support	Deadline
e.g. Research Skills	..become more familiar with sources of business information.	Speak to business students in my Halls of Residence.	Straight away! (this takes time)

Self-Marketing Tips

As always, if applying for an 'advertised' position it is important to thoroughly analyse the advertisement before you begin, to identify the skills that are explicitly required (some may be considered Essential and some Desirable but nevertheless they want them all!!).

So what reference to business or commercial awareness does the business make in the advertisement?

In carrying out your further research about the organisation, what mention do they make of business awareness? Why do you think it's so important in their business to demonstrate a high level of business awareness?

When making a speculative application to an organisation it is even more important that you are able to demonstrate your awareness of the issues currently facing the organisation and an in depth understanding of the organisation's existing operations. When asked the question about why you chose to approach them you will be in a sound position to explain what has attracted you to them as a potential employer.

Interview Questions

As impossible as it may seem, trying to 'guess' the kind of interview questions you may face and preparing answers for them is actually a valuable preparation for the interview. In the same way, when faced by an essay in examination conditions, if you have drafted some possible answers in advance your fluency is improved, you will respond more coherently and cohesively overall.

Self-Marketing Tips

The kind of questions you may face to assess your business awareness may be as follows:

- What do you know about our organisation?
- Why do you wish to enter the .... industry?
- What are our main products/services?
- What are the problems facing our industry at this time?
- What changes have there been in our industry recently?
- Who are our competitors? What are the differences between them and us?
- Who are our clients?
- What do you think the job you would be doing entails?
- Where do you see yourself in 5 years' time?
- What salary do you expect?
- How do you keep up to date with what is going on in business?
- What story in the business press has interested you most recently?
- What is the current Bank of England base rate?
- How many euros would you get today in exchange for £10?
- What is the FTSE 100? Did the FTSE go up or down yesterday?
- What was our share price this morning?

Self-Marketing Tips

You may even be asked during the interview to make a short presentation on a particular topic related to the business (you are normally given the topic in advance) or you may even be asked 'on the spot' to talk for X minutes about the business. Preparing for this element of the recruitment process will require real business awareness and a degree of flair in presenting the information – remember if the recruiting team are interviewing more than a couple of applicants they may have heard it all before that day! How can you make sure the way you demonstrate your business awareness sets you apart from the other applicants?

CHAPTER 3

Problem Solving and Decision Making

Step 1

Review

"The ability to problem solve is a major requirement for many roles within our business, be it R&D, logistics, finance, sales, IT, marketing, etc. A graduate should be able to demonstrate their ability to identify, analyse and formulate a solution to a problem, since it is likely to play a large part of their day-to-day work."

Anthony Hudson, Senior Manager at ISCA (via GO Wales)

What is Problem Solving?

Problem solving is something we do every day, in our studies, at work and in our day-to-day lives.

Some of the problems that you may typically face include:

- putting together an argument for an essay
- debugging a computer program
- dealing with an awkward customer when working part-time in a shop or restaurant
- thinking about how you are going to manage your budget to keep you going until the end of term
- working out why your printer won't respond
- developing a strategy to reach the next level of a computer game.

Any role will also bring problems to be faced. It is important to show to a recruiter that you have the right skills to resolve these problems, and the personal qualities to handle the challenges and pressure they may bring.

In simple terms, you need to be able to:

- evaluate information or situations
- break them down into their key components
- consider various ways of approaching and resolving them
- decide on the most appropriate of these ways (we will turn to 'decision making' later in the chapter).

One of the key skills required when problem solving is how to handle conflict. Problem solving is all about looking at situations in new and different ways and for many people this can be unsettling, particularly if the solution to the problem requires change.

Learning the skills to handle conflict is often overlooked during a degree programme; that's not to say you won't have experienced conflict but sadly it would be a pretty exceptional university that taught its students the necessary skills to deal with it. However, employers commonly cite conflict management as being a critical requirement when recruiting. Therefore, within this text we explore the skill of "conflict management" and in the next chapter attempt to begin to address this potential skill gap.

The reality after all is that businesses are operating in an increasingly complex world. Globalisation and technology have opened up new markets and enabled new competitors. With an abundance of options to choose from, customers are harder to please – and more fickle – than ever. Each day competitive advantage seems more elusive and fleeting. Even if they can figure out the right approach to take, what works today won't work tomorrow.

The growth of complexity is also often reflected in businesses' goals. According to the Boston Consulting Group (http://www.bcg.com/), today companies, on average, set themselves six times as many performance requirements as they did in 1955, the year the Fortune 500 list was created. Back then, Chief Executive Officers committed to four to seven performance imperatives; today they commit to 25 to 40. And many of those requirements appear to be in conflict: companies that want to satisfy their customers, who demand low prices and high quality. Brand Managers who seek to customise their offerings for specific markets and standardize them for the greatest operating return. And everyone wanting to innovate and be efficient.

>>

<<

In and of itself, this complexity is not a bad thing – it brings opportunities as well as challenges. The problem is the way businesses attempt to respond to it. To reconcile their many conflicting goals, managers redesign the organisation's structure, performance measures, and incentives, trying to align employees' behaviour with shifting external challenges. More layers get added, more procedures and policies imposed. Then, to smooth the implementation of those "hard" changes, companies introduce a variety of "soft" initiatives designed to infuse work with positive emotions and create a workplace where interpersonal relationships and collaboration will flourish.

As you can see, working within this increasingly complex environment requires real problem solving skills and the ability to manage conflict as it arises.

As part of the problem solving challenge, decisions need to be made and this in itself requires a particular skill set that is highly desirable to business.

If we follow the simple method of problem solving outlined above, by the time you reach the decision making stage you should have a list of alternative solutions. Producing a short list of the best options is the next critical stage. Start by removing any obviously poorer choices. Try not to have too many options in your final list (it is a SHORT list after all!) or it will be too confusing. Next differentiate between practical and impractical solutions: what CAN be achieved given the resources available?

Finally it's time to make your decision. For each of your shortlist of options consider its advantages and disadvantages. Try to recognise any inconsistencies in your reasoning and question any assumptions you have made. Identify the key factors that will shape your decision and then evaluate each option against the key factors to consider the combined effect of all the factors. By the time you have done this it is likely that one option or solution will become favourite but if not then assign a priority to each factor and re-evaluate. If you are still in a position where two (or even more) options are looking good then consider yourself lucky – you have a 'Plan B' and maybe even a 'Plan C'!

>>

1. Problem Solving

There are many models available to assist us in problem solving. One of the most simplistic (but effective) is the IDEAL model.

The model has five key steps.

- **I**dentify the problem
- **D**efine the problem
- **E**xamine the options
- **A**ct on a plan
- **L**ook at the consequences

A more detailed model such as the following may be useful to consider in the early stages of your development of these skills.

1. **Evaluating the problem**
   - **Clarifying** the nature of a problem
   - **Formulating** questions
   - **Gathering** information systematically
   - **Collating** and organising data
   - **Condensing** and summarising information
   - **Defining** the desired objective
2. **Managing the problem**
   - **Using the information gathered** effectively
   - **Breaking down a problem** into smaller, more manageable, parts
   - Using techniques such as **brainstorming** and lateral thinking to consider options
   - **Analysing these options** in greater depth
   - **Identifying steps that can be taken** to achieve the objective

3. **Decision making**
   - **Deciding between the possible options** for what action to take
   - **Deciding on further information** to be gathered before taking action
   - **Deciding on resources** (time, funding, staff etc) to be allocated to this problem
4. **Resolving the problem**
   - **Implementing action**
   - **Providing information** to other stakeholders; delegating tasks
   - Reviewing progress
5. **Examining the results**
   - **Monitoring the outcome** of the action take
   - **Reviewing the problem and problem-solving process** to avoid similar situations in future

As you can see, problem solving can itself be a complex process with multiple stakeholders involved. Managing the process and any conflict that arises as a result is critical to its success. When managing conflict you may like to consider the following tips.

1. **Focus on behaviour and not on your interpretations**

   For example, just because someone is talking loudly and gesticulating does not necessarily mean they are angry – maybe they are excited? We can never truly know how someone is feeling or thinking so don't try to second guess this:

2. **Avoid the use of "always" and "never"**

   Using imperatives like this can be inflammatory. It is highly unlikely that someone will ever display that kind of consistency in their actions that you can truly claim they 'always' or 'never' behave in a certain way.

3. **Use "I" statements**

   At some point in the conflict conversation, you will eventually need

to address your interpretations of their behaviour. When this time comes, phrase your interpretation in the form of an "I" statement. Using the behaviour mentioned above as an example, you could say something like:

- "When you speak loudly, I feel like you are angry with me," instead of "Why are you so angry!"
- "When you speak that directly, I feel threatened," instead of "Why are you threatening me?"

4. **Say what you want rather than what you don't want**

   If you would like someone to change their behaviour towards you, tell them what you would like to see rather than what you don't want to see. When we tell someone what not to do in a relationship, we fail to clarify what we want to see instead. For example, you could say, "When you speak to me, please lower the volume." rather than "Stop shouting at me!"

5. **Beware of your non-verbal messages**

   Remember that the other person will respond negatively to anything you do that they perceive negatively (aggressive, threatening, dismissive, disrespectful, etc.). Calmly maintain steady eye-contact, relaxed posture, and a calm voice tone and you will improve your communication during conflict.

6. **Apologise for your contribution**

   Conflicts rarely happen entirely because of one person's actions. If only unintentionally, you probably did something to frustrate or irritate the other person in the moments just prior to or just after the conflict began. Go ahead and apologise. It won't harm you or diminish you. On the contrary, it will probably strengthen your status with the other person.

7. **Give them a chance to speak**

   People need to be heard and understood. If you will slow down long enough to really listen to them, they will probably calm down enough to listen to you. When people get a chance to say what is on their mind, they experience what psychologists call catharsis (or cleansing). This cleansing helps to lower emotional energy and pave the way for a more productive dialogue.

<<

One final tip...

Problem solving is NOT necessarily a linear process. You cannot expect to start at 'Stage 1' and move methodically through to the final stage each time. On occasion you may need to move back a stage because you uncover new information or new factors have come to light. Sometimes you may even need to start right back at the beginning! This is one of the challenges and opportunities of problem solving; to demonstrate the professional resilience to handle this positively with an 'eye on the prize'!

2. Decision Making

As covered in the chapter introduction, a critical stage of the decision making process is to identify the factors that are important in making the decision and then to evaluate the options, or potential solutions, using these factors.

Two ways in which might undertake this stage are covered below.

A Decision Matrix

How to construct your decision matrix.

1. Take your short list of options/solutions
2. Identify the factors that will shape or influence your decision (See Column 1)
3. Weight each factor in terms of importance (See Column 2 i.e. x?)
4. Score each option/solution (See Columns 3, 4 and 5)
5. Apply the weighting (See Columns 3, 4 and 5)
6. Calculate the total score for each option. (See Final Row)

>>

<<

Here's an example.

Which career would be most suitable for me? Teacher, Actor or Sales Executive.				
Factor	**Weighting**	**Teacher**	**Actor**	**Sales Executive**
Job Security	High (x3)	9 (x3) = 27	1 (x3) = 3	4 (x3) = 12
Informal Working Environment	Low (x1)	4 (x1) = 4	8 (x1) = 8	2 (x1) = 2
9 to 5 Work	Low (x1)	2 (x1) = 1	1 (x1) = 1	8 (x1) = 8
Good Salary	High (x3)	4 (x3) = 12	2 (x3) = 6	6 (x3) = 18
Job Satisfaction	Medium (x2)	8 (x2) = 16	8 (x2) = 16	4 (x2) = 8
TOTAL	**n/a**	**60**	**34**	**48**

So applying this technique would suggest that the decision to be made for this person is to pursue a career as a teacher (it scored most highly).

SWOT Analysis

SWOT is another method of analysing and evaluating an option or solution.

S = Strengths

W = Weaknesses

O = Opportunities

T = Threats

Each option/solution would be evaluated in a separate SWOT and then they would be compared and contrasted to identify the optimum solution.

>>

<<

SWOT is normally presented as follows.

Strengths	Weaknesses
Opportunities	Threats

Each quadrant would be populated with the relevant points pertaining to the option being evaluated.

Step 2

Assess

Use the following tool to assess your problem solving skills.

We are going to apply the IDEAL model of problem solving.

The model has five key steps.

- **I**dentify the problem
- **D**efine the problem
- **E**xamine the options
- **A**ct on a plan
- **L**ook at the consequences

>>

Identify the problem

Choose a problem that you are currently facing.

The problem that I am currently facing is...

Define the problem

Explore the problem more fully. For example:

The problem has arisen because...

The people involved in the problem are...

The problem needs to be resolved by (insert date)...

Other comments

<<

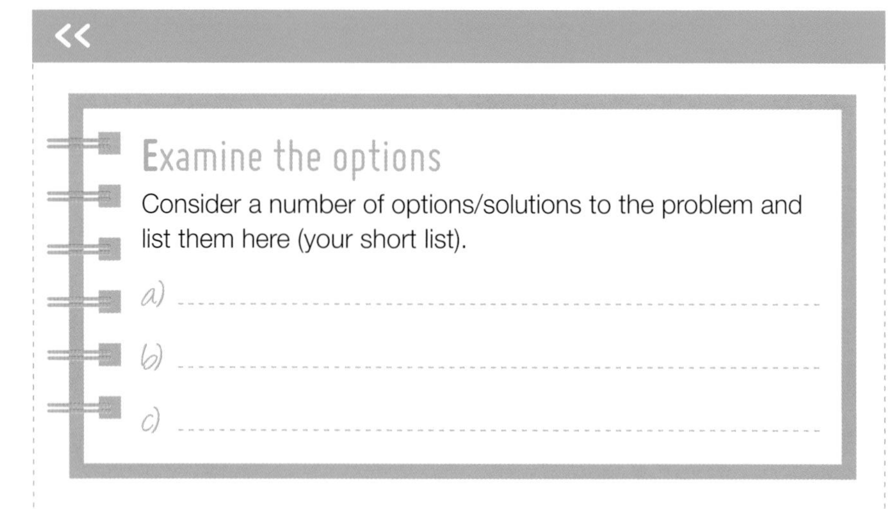

Examine the options

Consider a number of options/solutions to the problem and list them here (your short list).

a) ....

b) ....

c) ....

Act on a plan

Time to make a decision! Construct a decision matrix or series of SWOT analyses to evaluate your options.

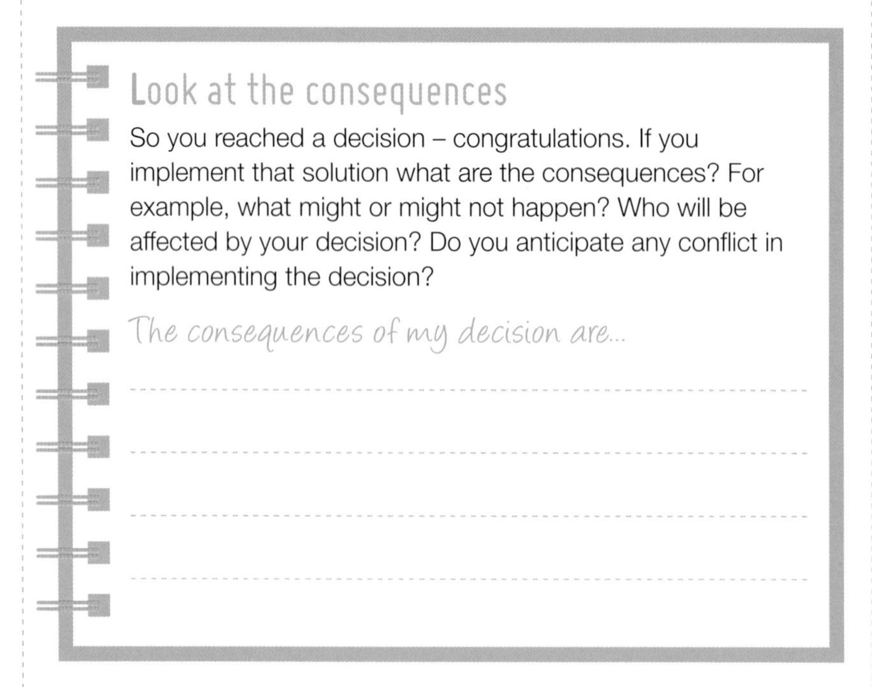

Look at the consequences

So you reached a decision – congratulations. If you implement that solution what are the consequences? For example, what might or might not happen? Who will be affected by your decision? Do you anticipate any conflict in implementing the decision?

The consequences of my decision are...

....

....

....

....

REMEMBER – The more thoroughly you engage with this stage the more value you will gain from this whole process.

Step 3

Application (how might skill be applied)

When asked about problem solving skills, CogNexus founder Jeff Conklin suggested that the current education system is only preparing students to deal with what he calls 'tame' problems. But in reality business today faces 'wicked' problems (his description), which are unexpected and can cause havoc. He recommends that the solution to this problem solving 'problem' is to achieve a shared understanding of the problem amongst all stakeholders. He comments that it is only by achieving this level of understanding (a detailed, in-depth exploration of the problem from multiple perspectives) that 'wicked' problems can be resolved. Central to this is the development of effective communication between stakeholders and the management of conflict should it arise.

According to Bridget Webber, writing in Helium Knowledge, there is a definite link between problem solving and career advancement. Her research indicates that individuals who are at the head of companies and earn the most money are effective solution finders and may be described as ideas people. Bridget describes them as individuals who think about problems deeply, and learn by experience. Sometimes they use their heads and are practical, and at other times they rely on a gut feeling that tells them how to turn a bad situation around. In her opinion, instinct about how to solve problems tends to be gained via learning and experiencing difficult situations.

Instinct is an interesting 'element' or 'factor' at play in problem solving and decision making and has been the subject of quite a degree of critical thought in recent years. Although considered by many to be highly unscientific and therefore largely unmeasurable, there is a growing body of thought around the positive value of instinct in problem solving and decision making.

It may be worthwhile to suggest that 'instinct' forms one of the factors that you employ when evaluating options or solutions. What is your 'gut feel', what is your instinct telling you? Of course, this all requires you to have developed an instinct to achieve this!

Step 4

Reflect (what have I learned?)

STOP!

By now you are likely to have gained a considerable amount of information about problem solving and decision making. By carrying out the problem solving exercise in Step 2 you will have had the opportunity to test out your skills in this area. It is also worthwhile to reflect on other experiences you have had of problem solving and decision making. For example, experiences during your studies, other work experience you may have gained and by working through this chapter. Let's take some time to make sense of it all.

Task 1

Reflect on the problem solving exercise in Step 2 and write a paragraph (or two!) describing the experience below.

Focus on the IDEAL model in your writing.

Was any part of the IDEAL model more difficult than any other, if so why?

How could you address these difficulties? Does it involve you developing your skills further or getting more practice (or both)?

>>

What are the strengths and weaknesses of this model?

How do you think this model would work in a business setting?

Is this example 'typical' of your problem solving and decision making experience? If not, what makes it different?

<<

Task 2

Looking back on this and other experiences of problem solving and decision making you've had, how do you feel about problem solving and decision making?

Task 3

Re-read your answers to Tasks 1 and 2 above. Does anything you've written surprise you?

>>

Now you've nearly reached the end of this chapter, what do you think you've learnt about this area and yourself as a problem solver and decision maker?

If you are finding this difficult, imagine that you are commenting on someone else's answers to the Task 1 and 2 questions. What would you advise them about problem solving and decision making?

Step 5

Evaluate (reach a judgement on personal performance)

So the time has come. How do you judge/rate/score yourself at problem solving and decision making? Use the information from this chapter and the previous steps to inform your decision.

Score yourself using a scale of 0 – 10 where 0 = No Skills and 10 = Highly Skilled.

Score:

Return to the Self-Assessment you undertook at the end of Chapter 1 and note the score you gave yourself then for problem solving and decision making.

Self-Assessment Score:

Step 6

Check List (what next...future development)

Skill: Problem Solving and Decision Making			
Area for Improvement	**I need to.....**	**Sources of Support**	**Deadline**
e.g. Conflict management	..make more use of ‘I’ statements when giving feedback.	I can practise this with trusted friends.	Insert Date

Self-Marketing Tips

As always, if applying for an 'advertised' position it is important to thoroughly analyse the advertisement before you begin; to identify the skills that are explicitly required (some may be considered Essential and some Desirable but nevertheless they want them all!!)

So what reference to problem solving and decision making do they make in the advertisement?

In carrying out your further research about the organisation, what mention do they make of problem solving and decision-making? Are there examples on their website or annual report of recent problems they've overcome? See if you can speak to one of their existing employees and ask about how they solve problems and reach decisions. What language do they use in talking about the value of problem solving and decision making?

By 'mirroring' the way in which the organisation use language to discuss a skill set you are making the job of the HR person or recruiting manager that much easier when reading your application.

If you are making a speculative application to the organisation then the same approach is equally valuable. You won't have an advertisement or job description to work from but with some diligent research you can learn a great deal about the organisation's approach to and perspective on problem solving and decision making which you can then reflect in your application.

Your Portfolio

As part of your self-marketing strategy you are encouraged to make a career-long commitment to building a portfolio of evidence, a copy of which can either accompany applications or be taken to meetings and interviews for review by the recruiter. This needs to be regularly updated, certainly at least each time you take on a new position.

In your portfolio you might include anything that demonstrates your experience, skills and competencies. For example:

- CV/resume
- references
- testimonials
- feedback/Reviews (360 Degree – from peers, supervisors and your staff)
- examples of work carried out (academic or work-related e.g. reports, presentations, multimedia)
- qualification/degree certificates.

Within your portfolio you could include an example of a problem solving exercise you undertook at college/ university.

Undertake a SWOT analysis of the business to which you are applying; this demonstrates not only that you have the skills to apply this tool but that you have also developed an in-depth body of knowledge about the organisation.

“Record your achievements and be prepared to speak about them.”

Daniel Merriott, IS and Business Consultant
(www.danielmerriott.net)

CHAPTER 4
Dealing with Conflict and Stress

Step 1

Review

What is Conflict Management?

According to research by Thomas and Schmidt up to 30% of a typical manager's time is spent dealing with conflict. This kind of statistic might at first fill us with dread about the modern day workplace. However, there is an argument to suggest that avoiding conflict is not only impossible but also undesirable.

As discussed briefly in the previous chapter, conflict is often a 'by-product' of change and change is almost inevitable in the modern workplace. With this in mind then an effective employee needs to embrace conflict and co-create an environment where differences of perspective can be discussed and a win-win outcome created.

The management of conflict requires a high level of self-leadership (self management) as well as excellent communication skills.

The previous chapter discussed the fact that one of the key skills required when problem solving is also how to handle conflict. Problem solving is all about looking at situations in new and different ways and for many people this can be unsettling, particularly if the solution to the problem requires change. However, change itself can also be a cause of workplace stress.

What is Stress?

Workplace stress is commonly defined as the harmful physical and emotional response that occurs when there is a poor match between job demands and the capabilities, resources or needs of the worker.

Individuals suffering from stress often display a range of signs that may be noticed by colleagues and other managers.

These signs include:

- tiredness and irritability
- reduced quality of work

>>

- indecisiveness and poor judgement
- loss of sense of humour
- physical illness such as headaches, nausea, aches and pains
- seeming jumpy or ill-at-ease, or admitting to sleeping badly
- increased sick leave
- poor timekeeping
- changes in working day patterns - perhaps by staying late or taking work home.

You might also witness signs of more widespread problems among groups of employees, for example:

- arguments and disputes between staff
- general absenteeism
- an increase in grievances and complaints
- greater staff turnover.

Conflict in the workplace is a common cause of work-related stress and therefore developing the skills to manage conflict more effectively can certainly contribute to the reduction of workplace stress.

1. Conflict Management

Conflict can occur in a variety of shapes and forms. However, in this chapter we will be dealing with conflict between individuals and conflict between groups.

Managing conflict between individuals

It is recommended that when a conflict arises you should try to take a calm approach and not react in a challenging way. It is also best not to ignore the problem and hope that it will go away. The best way to handle conflict is to face it and have a planned approach.

If the business you are working for has policies or procedures in place, you can use these to determine how to approach the issue. It may also

help to have an employee representative and/or a senior manager to support you if:

- you find it difficult to confront your managers and make a complaint
- you are managing a number of individuals with whom you have conflict.

Following are a set of recommendations as to how you might deal with this form of conflict.

Talk informally

Everyone involved should have an opportunity to have their say. Everyone in the business should know whom they can go to when they have issues and that they will be taken seriously.

Investigate formally

It is important that the individual managing the situation makes an informed decision by gathering information from everyone involved. They should think about what would be the best outcome for everyone involved, including the business itself.

Use internal procedures

Businesses should make sure that their grievance procedures are up to date and communicated to all staff, discussed at team meetings and at individual appraisals. These procedures will also help deal with issues such as bullying, absence and misconduct.

Upgrade the skills

Having one-to-one conversations requires sensitivity and empathy. Everyone should make sure that they:

- listen to what another employee says
- question them calmly to understand any underlying problems
- consider problems from a variety of perspectives
- lead by example
- comply with the latest employment laws
- have up-to-date policies on dispute resolution procedures.

>>

Get external help

Resolving personal conflicts can be difficult if an individual feels they are too close to the problem. Therefore, there are a range of external options that can be considered in these circumstances.

In the UK, one of the most commonly used external options is ACAS (Advisory, Conciliation and Arbitration Service) that can help by providing mediation. This involves an independent, impartial person helping two or more individuals or groups to discuss their problems and reach a solution that's acceptable to everyone.

Managing conflict between groups

Sometimes businesses do have to make difficult decisions about work practices, pay and organisational rules and procedures, all of which may cause conflict.

Here are some ideas about how to avoid or address conflict between groups.

- Communication
  - Ensure that all communication is relevant, concise and delivered in a suitable way. Employees should be consulted before decisions are made.
- Representative structures – if you can't talk to each person individually, set up 'sounding boards' of employee representatives:
  - set up working groups to consider issues such as absence levels
  - develop staff councils or consultative committees to look at issues like new products and training
  - involve trade union representatives to negotiate terms and conditions of employment.

>>

<<

2. Stress

As discussed, conflict can be a common cause of stress in the workplace but there are a number of other common factors also.

Some typical stress inducers

- Excessively **high workloads**, with unrealistic deadlines making people feel rushed, under pressure and overwhelmed.
- **Insufficient workloads**, making people feel that their skills are being underused.
- A **lack of control** over work activities.
- A lack of interpersonal support or poor working relationships leading to a sense of isolation.
- People being asked to do a job for which they have insufficient experience or training.
- Difficulty settling into a new promotion, both in terms of meeting the new role's requirements and adapting to possible changes in relationships with colleagues.
- Concerns about job security, lack of career opportunities, or level of pay.
- **Bullying or harassment**.
- A **blame culture** within your business where people are afraid to get things wrong or to admit to making mistakes.
- **Weak or ineffective management** which leaves employees feeling they don't have a sense of direction, or **over-management**, which can leave employees feeling undervalued and affect their self-esteem.
- Multiple reporting lines for employees, with each manager asking for their work to be prioritised.
- Failure to keep employees informed about significant changes to the business, causing them uncertainty about their future.
- A **poor physical working environment**, e.g. excessive heat, cold or noise, inadequate lighting, uncomfortable seating, malfunctioning equipment, etc.

>>

Tackling the causes of work-related stress

Once the possible stress problems in the business have been identified, steps can then be taken to tackle the causes.

- If overwork is causing people to feel stressed, the business should consider how to reduce their workload and ensure targets are challenging but realistic. Staff should be helped to prioritise work, cutting out unnecessary tasks, and provided with time-management training if necessary. The delegation of work where possible should be encouraged.
- Staff must take their holiday entitlement.
- Individuals should be well-matched to the jobs they are given. Make sure the business' recruitment and selection procedures help them to achieve this.
- Every employee should have a well-defined role - and should know what it is.
- Staff performance should be reviewed so that they know how they're doing and the business can identify any training they may need.
- Employees should be given more autonomy where possible, allowing them to plan their work schedule and decide how to tackle problems.
- The management style should encourage employees to discuss problems with their managers and provide them with opportunities to feed back or express ideas about their work.
- Staff should be kept informed about the business' direction and should be told about significant changes to the business.
- The business should have effective disciplinary and grievance procedures to tackle bullying and harassment.

As discussed in the introduction to the chapter, workplace stress can have hugely adverse affects on an individual's physical and psychological well-being. Ensure you are prepared to identify the causes of stress and have the skills required to address it.

>>

Step 2

Assess

Identifying stress in colleagues is often easier than recognising when you are personally stressed. Take a couple of minutes to think about your own 'stress flags': those symptoms that tell you when you are suffering from stress in the workplace.

Think back to a time when you have been recognisably stressed recently. Maybe you were up against an assessment deadline at university or college? Maybe your employer has asked you to do some extra shifts which meant you had less time for your studies and you felt unable to say no!

Take a look at the list of symptoms in the first column below and then mark with a tick or a cross if you exhibited that symptom during the experience you described above.

Frequency	Never	Sometimes	Often	Always
Symptom				
Reduced quality of work				
Loss of sense of humour				
Headaches				

>>

Nausea				
Aches and pains				
Poor sleep habits				
Absence from work/uni/ college				
Poor timekeeping				
Behaving in an argumentative manner				
Displaying poor judgement				
Lacking concentration				
Depressed				

Which of these symptoms did you exhibit most frequently during this experience? Note them below.

Step 3

Application (how might skill be applied)

The Head of Safety, Health and Wellbeing at Leeds Metropolitan University, John Hamilton, when interviewed stated that results of their new scheme to tackle workplace stress includes the fact that the university now saves £75,000 a year in wages. Stress-related absence is down by 16% and the accident rate is now at just 64.7 per 100,000 employees, compared to the sector average of 325. So not only is the scheme a welcome benefit for employees but it also makes commercial sense for the organisation.

According to a recent report from Aviva UK Health one in three employees are known to skip their lunch break and yet it is well documented that taking regular breaks boosts morale and efficiency. The same report found that only 43% of managers encourage their staff to take lunch breaks and therefore one of the key report recommendations is that managers encourage staff to take breaks and that in-house catering offers healthy options to improve staff well-being.

Needless to say, in a performance-driven business environment highlighting the importance of employee well-being and its affect on performance can be a challenge, although there is certainly more evidence in the UK that employers are beginning to understand the significance of this. The reality of course can be very different; when a crucial deadline looms and there aren't enough hours in the day to meet the customer's expectations then sadly lunch is often the last option. On occasion maybe this is something that can be tolerated by all but if it becomes a regular, even typical, experience then it needs to be addressed not only for your personal well-being, but because of your performance and therefore its impact on the business.

You might gather evidence over a month about your breaks (or lack of them!) and performance so that your manager or employer can clearly see the issue. Bring them a solution too – not just the problem! How can your break time be protected? How will this improve your performance and stress levels and ultimately affect the business?

If this is not addressed, as with other issues in the workplace, you may need to refer to company policy (if it exists) or escalate to more senior management.

Step 4

Reflect (what have I learned?)

STOP!

By now you are likely to have gained a considerable amount of information about dealing with conflict and stress. By carrying out the exercise in Step 2 you will have had the opportunity to consider your own 'stress flags' during one stressful experience.

It is also worthwhile to reflect on other stressful experiences you have had and how you reacted during those periods. For example, experiences during your studies, other work experience you may have gained and by working through this chapter. Let's take some time to make sense of it all.

Task 1

Reflect on the exercise in Step 2 and write a paragraph (or two!) describing the experience below.

Was it difficult to remember a stressful experience accurately?

Do you consider yourself to be a person who commonly suffers from stress?

Were your symptoms easy to identify?

Do you think the symptoms you identified are typical of your response to stress? If not, what makes it different?

Task 2

Looking back on this and other experiences of conflict and stress you've had, how do you feel about these two areas?

Task 3

Re-read your answers to Tasks 1 and 2 above. Does anything you've written surprise you?

Now you've nearly reached the end of this chapter, what do you think you've learnt about this area and yourself with regard to conflict management and stress in the workplace?

If you are finding this difficult, imagine that you are commenting on someone else's answers to the Task 1 and 2 questions. What would you advise them about conflict management and stress?

Step 5

Evaluate (reach a judgement on personal performance)

So the time has come. How do you judge/rate/score yourself at conflict and stress management? Use the information from this chapter and the previous steps to inform your decision.

Score yourself using a scale of 0 – 10 where 0 = No Skills and 10 = Highly Skilled.

Score:

Return to the Self-Assessment you undertook at the end of Chapter 1 and note the score you gave yourself then for conflict and stress management.

Self-Assessment Score:

Step 6

Check List (what next...future development)

Skill: Dealing with conflict and stress

Area for Improvement	I need to.....	Sources of Support	Deadline
e.g. Stress Management	..plan my work-load and prioritise better	Talk to my tutor/manager about this.	Insert Date

Self-Marketing Tips

As always, if applying for an 'advertised' position it is important to thoroughly analyse the advertisement before you begin; to identify the skills that are explicitly required (some may be considered Essential and some Desirable but nevertheless they want them all!!).

So what reference to conflict management and sources of stress do they make in the advertisement?

In carrying out your further research about the organisation, what mention do they make of potential sources of conflict and stress? Do they talk about their policies and approach to employee well-being? Are there examples on their website or annual report of steps they've taken to improve employee well-being? See if you can speak to one of their existing employees and ask about how they handle stress and conflict in the workplace.

By 'mirroring' the way in which the organisation use language to discuss a skill set you are making the job of the HR person or recruiting manager that much easier when reading your application.

If you are making a speculative application to the organisation then the same approach is equally valuable. You won't have an advertisement or job description to work from but with some diligent research you can learn a great deal about the organisation's approach to and perspective on employee well-being which you can then reflect in your application.

Assessment Centres

As part of the recruitment process you may be invited to participate in an 'assessment centre'.

Self-Marketing Tips

They may last one or two days or even longer and are usually held after the first round of interviews and before the final selection. They may also be used as an initial selection process. You will be asked to engage in a number of activities and exercises during which multiple assessors will observe and rate your performance.

Assessment centres are particularly useful for businesses to evaluate an applicant's behaviour and reaction to certain scenarios. In terms of conflict management and dealing with stress, an assessment centre is an important opportunity for a potential employer to observe applicants' abilities in these areas.

Assessment centres typically include a number of elements.

- Social/informal events: where you meet a variety of people, including other candidates, the assessors, recent graduates and the wider staff and management team. Be aware that you are being assessed at all times. Be friendly but not over-familiar.
- Information sessions: provide more detail about the organisation and the roles available. Listen carefully, as the information provided may be useful during the rest of the day.
- Tests and exercises: designed to reveal your ability and potential. Assessors measure you against a set of competencies. Each exercise is designed to assess one or more of these areas. You may be put into a stressful scenario, where for example you are managing a conflict between two more junior members of staff. Prepare to demonstrate you have the skills to handle the stress involved and that you can manage conflict effectively.

Self-Marketing Tips

“I firmly believe the confidence to sell yourself, if not present before you go to university, can be learnt. Merely the act of interacting with lots of different people will help. For example friends in the sports team may be different from those you make on your course. Ensuring you interact with people from all backgrounds will help you communicate in an interview, especially if you are nervous, and are intimated by those who are interviewing you.”

Mona Chergui, Human Resources Officer, www.msc.org

CHAPTER 5
Numeracy

Step 1

Review

What is Numeracy?

Numeracy is one of the key skills required in most workplaces. Working in industry, by its very nature, demands a certain degree of numerate ability and employers typically require some form of data handling skills to be demonstrated by applicants.

Examples

- When recording data, applicants should organise and record it fully and accurately.
- When processing data, applicants should:
    - make decisions about which data and calculations to use for the task
    - carry out calculations to appropriate levels of accuracy
    - check calculations, allow for possible errors and minimise their effects.
- When interpreting and presenting findings, applicants should:
    - select and use appropriate techniques to present clearly the main features of their findings, to appropriate levels of accuracy
    - describe and interpret their findings, allowing for possible sources of error.

Most people gain basic numeracy skills at school. These skills are used to a greater or lesser extent in daily life in shops, work and other situations. However, many people do not regard numeracy as important when trying to secure employment.

Nonetheless, a study conducted in 1993 for the Manpower Agency found that only one in eight jobs did not require any numeracy skills at all, with one in four requiring basic numeracy skills.

Interestingly, whilst employers report that basic skills such as numeracy are becoming increasingly important, a quarter also report that skill levels of applicants are only adequate (or worse).

>>

Here are some facts from research done by Skills Active which highlights the situation:

- 23% of adults in work in England struggle with maths or English
- 49 out of 50 jobs are closed to people with low literacy and numeracy skills
- 4 out of 5 jobs created now will require skill levels above A-level and only one third of Britons have these
- 6.8m adults are estimated to have difficulties in adding/subtracting using 3 digit numbers
- a total of 15m adults have skills at the same low level and have difficulties with fractions, decimals and simple percentages.

It is also fair to say that just because you have a university degree it does not necessarily mean you are numerate: you may not have anything higher in maths than a Grade C GCSE which could have been gained 5+ years ago!

It is important that you acknowledge the fact that you cannot 'avoid' numeracy any longer. If this is a 'weakness' in your portfolio it needs to be addressed immediately!

What are the Key Numeracy Skills?

If it's been a long while since you studied any mathematics or needed to do any calculations it may be worthwhile brushing up on these skills before the recruitment process begins. There are many sources of support online and some great sites that offer tutorial guidance also. Equally, you may well have sources of support within your University (talk to your careers service) or within your community – the local library is usually a good source of information about programmes in the area.

So what are the types of numeracy skills typically used in the workplace? Whilst the following is by no means an exhaustive list, it highlights areas where mistakes frequently occur.

1. **Percentages**

    - % change causes problems
      It is the change divided by the first number x100
      e.g. % change in price from 1997 to 1998
      1998 £20
      1997 £25

      Answer: Change = -£5 First no. is 1997 (£25)
      $\%\text{Change} = \frac{-£5}{£25} \times 100$
      = - 20%

2. **Averages**

    - Make sure you know the difference between:
        - the Arithmetic Mean (Average)
        - the Mode (Most frequently occurring)
        - the Median (Middle or 50% number)

          e.g. 4 4 5 8 9 12 18
          Mean = 60/7 = 8.57
          Mode = 4
          Median= 8
    - Know when to use each

3. **Graph work**

    - Remind yourself of different types of graph - especially the difference between a Bar Graph and a Histogram.
    - The Divided Bar Graph is frequently used - check it!
    - Gradients - increasing, decreasing, positive, negative and constant. Sketch these!
    - Trends - even though a line graph may have peaks and troughs, the start and finish gives the overall trend.
    - Moving Averages smooth out 'freak' results
    - Forecasting - the line of best fit and extrapolation will give a rough estimate.
    - Equation of a straight line - know it and use it!

>>

4. Charts and Diagrams

We sometimes use charts and diagrams to:

- read a bus timetable
- complete a table in a catalogue to buy goods
- draw up a floor plan.

Understanding charts and diagrams will help you to use them.

Some of us may have a road map book of the UK. We sometimes use them to find our way from one place to another. You will often find a mileage chart at the front of the book, in a diary or an exercise book. Practice using these.

What is the distance from Birmingham to London?

	B'ham	Cardiff	Edinburgh	London	York
B'ham		102	290	111	129
Cardiff	102		273	150	231
Edinburgh	290	373		372	186
London	111	150	372		194
York	129	231	186	194	

- Find the names of the two cities along the edge of the table.
- Make a note of which city is on top of the chart. You track DOWN the column from this one.
- At the same time, note where the other city is. From this, you track to the RIGHT along the row.
- It helps to use your fingers!
- You will find the correct answer where your fingers meet.

The distance between Birmingham and London is 111 miles.

>>

5. Algebra

- Use it! It can be helpful in solving arithmetical problems

e.g. If £1 = $2 and £1 = 10F, What does $1 equal in francs?

£1 = $2 =10F

$2 divided by 2 = $1

10F divided by 2 = 5F

$1 = 5F

6. Recording money

Prices can be marked on goods, or spoken, in different ways, for example:

Money written in figures is always written with two decimal places. The decimal point marks the end of the whole numbers, and the two columns on the right are for the pence.

Price A above would be recorded as £60.00, using two **trailing zeroes** to record that there are no pence.

The items in example B would be recorded as £0.85, £0.90 and £0.50. The **leading zero** is used when there are no whole numbers.

C would be recorded as £5.05, not as £5.5. The zero here is a **place holder**, so that the value of the five goes in the correct column (it is 5 hundredths or 5 pence).

If you use a calculator for money questions, you need to know that it **will not add trailing zeroes**, so an answer of twenty pounds sixty pence would appear as 20.6; you need to record it as £20.60.

The **key** to numerical competence is confidence and confidence is gained through practice - you can't 'swot up' at the last minute on mathematical techniques.

Step 2

Assess

Unfortunately, we do not have the scope in this guide to assess the breadth and depth of your numeracy skills but once again there are many online resources to support you in this plus the face to face sources of support we mentioned earlier.

We will however assess one area of your numeracy skills because it is important to consider how this makes you feel. Are you already cringing at the thought of this or are you even thinking of skipping to the next chapter? Mathematics or numeracy is sadly one area which frightens a significant proportion of the population and is often avoided but I would ask you to give it a go and treat it as a learning exercise in itself. The first step in dealing with this kind of concern is acknowledging it…let's see if we can make that step together.

Understanding averages

The average (mean) is calculated by adding up the figures given and then dividing by the total number of figures:

Average = total amount/total number of figures

Example: Find the average of 2, 4 and 6.

Total amount is 2 + 4 + 6 = 12

There are three numbers so the average is 12/3 = 4

>>

<<

Calculate the average of these figures:

1. 5, 12, 7
2. 6, 9, 15
3. 21, 32, 28
4. 44, 37, 48, 35
5. 92, 76, 88, 80
6. 103, 98, 87, 95, 102
7. 1003, 989, 654, 1226

Now self mark your work using the answers below.

Answers:

1. 8
2. 10
3. 27
4. 41
5. 84
6. 97
7. 968

How many did you get correct?

Step 3

Application (how might skill be applied)

Just by doing a simple internet search of this topic you will unearth a myriad of articles bemoaning the state of numeracy skills, of employers 'desperate' to recruit employees who have even a basic level of functional numeracy which will enable them to perform their job function.

How far this media portrayal represents reality is not within the remit of this guide but in terms of your own approach to job seeking this is a CLEAR opportunity to shine!

>>

Ensuring you have and can demonstrate functional numeracy during and after the recruitment process would appear to put you ahead of a large percentage of the population if the reports are to be believed.

By reading job advertisements and job descriptions you will begin to get an understanding of the essential requirement to be numerate for most roles. Below is a job description from the manufacturing industry. Read through it and identify how many times numeracy skills are mentioned.

Logistics Manager : Job description

Logistics and distribution managers organise the storage and distribution of goods, which often involves using complex IT and telecommunications systems. They plan and manage the movement of goods in a supply chain, liaising with many parties including suppliers of raw materials, manufacturers, retailers and consumers.

Logistics and distribution managers need an awareness of and strategic response to external influences, such as legislation, fuel costs (1) and environmental pressures.

The role of a distribution manager within logistics may involve transportation, stock control (2), warehousing and ensuring structures are in place to monitor the flow of goods and materials. IT plays a key part within the logistics field in forecasting (3) increasingly complex systems of stock levels, delivery times (4), transport costs (5) and performance evaluation (6).

Typical work activities

Responsibilities vary according to the specific job role and whether the employing company is a manufacturer, retailer or specialist service provider (third party logistics or 3PL).

A range of business tasks is undertaken to support the smooth and efficient operation of supply chain processes, and typical work activities usually include:

- monitoring the quality, quantity, cost and efficiency of the movement and storage of goods (7)

>>

- coordinating and controlling the order cycle and associated information systems
- analysing data (8) to monitor performance and plan improvements and demand
- allocating and managing staff resources (9) according to changing needs
- liaising and negotiating (10) with customers and suppliers
- developing business by gaining new contracts, analysing logistical problems (11) and producing new solutions.

When managing warehouse or transport staff, the role may also include:

- implementing health and safety procedures
- managing staff training issues
- motivating other members of the team
- project management (12)
- setting objectives (13).

More senior roles in logistics may involve:

- planning projects
- using specialist knowledge, such as mechanical-handling systems, to provide consultancy services.

Do you agree with the 13 that we found or did you find more? Whatever your score, there is clearly a significant need for the person in this role to be numerate.

Step 4

Reflect (what have I learned?)

STOP!

By now you are likely to have gained a considerable amount of information that has enabled you to reflect on your numeracy skills.

Task 1

Reflect on the exercise in Step 2 and write a paragraph (or two!) describing the experience below.

How did you feel when you realised you were going to have to do some maths?

How do you feel about your result?

>>

Task 2

Looking back on this and other experiences of applying your numerical skills, how do you feel about your ability to perform these skills in the workplace?

Task 3

Re-read your answers to Tasks 1 and 2 above. Does anything you've written surprise you?

<<

Now you've nearly reached the end of this chapter, what do you think you've learnt about this area and yourself with regard to numeracy in the workplace?

If you are finding this difficult, imagine that you are commenting on someone else's answers to the Task 1 and 2 questions. What would you advise them about their numerical skills?

Step 5

Evaluate (reach a judgement on personal performance)

So the time has come. How do you judge/rate/score your numerical skills? Use the information from this chapter and the previous steps to inform your decision.

Score yourself using a scale of 0 – 10 where 0 = No Skills and 10 = Highly Skilled.

Score:

Return to the Self-Assessment you undertook at the end of Chapter 1 and note the score you gave yourself then for numeracy.

Self-Assessment Score:

Step 6

Check List (what next...future development)

Skill: Numeracy

Area for Improvement	I need to.....	Sources of Support	Deadline
e.g. Graphs	..make sure I can confidently create a variety of different graphs to display data.	Go to my careers service to find out about local classes.	Insert Date

Self-Marketing Tips

As previously mentioned, prospective employers may well be very keen to assess your level of numerical skills (particularly given the supposed 'concern' expressed by them in the media!). There are a number of ways in which they may choose to do this that you should be prepared to tackle.

It may be something as simple as a written test with a range of questions designed to test your ability to handle a number of different forms of calculation. Alternatively it could be a case study and in-tray or e-tray exercises, which are business simulation tasks.

This type of task is designed to examine a number of skills such as communication, organisational ability, problem-solving, data analysis, planning, time management and decision making. There is usually a time limit on these exercises and after the task you may be asked to justify your actions.

Case study exercises

In these exercises, you will be given a set of documents relating to a hypothetical or real-life situation. You are likely to be asked to analyse it and to give a brief verbal or written report of your recommendations.

You may be asked to complete the case study individually or as part of a group. Some employers will set case study exercises as a discrete element of the selection process. Others may combine them with an interview.

Tips for tackling a case study

- Practise with sample case studies in advance and brush up on your numeracy skills.

Self-Marketing Tips

- Research the organisation and its markets and be up to speed on current affairs.
- Read the instructions carefully and thoroughly.
- Read any background information you are given about the organisation, the staff and your role. Focus on key points and make brief notes. This will help you to get a feel for what is important.
- Scan through all items to get an overall view of everything that will need to be considered.
- Try to stay calm. Keep a note of the time to ensure you pace yourself correctly.
- Work as quickly and as accurately as you can.
- When presenting your conclusions or discussing your rationale be as clear as possible and don't be afraid to disagree with the selector if you feel you have made the right decision.

In-tray/e-tray exercises

These are business simulation exercises in which you are given an in-tray or electronic inbox full of emails, company memos, telephone and fax messages, reports and correspondence. You will be provided with information about the structure of the organisation and your place within it. You are expected to take decisions, prioritise your workload, draft replies, delegate tasks and recommend actions.

Each exercise is designed to test how you handle complex information within a limited time. It allows you to demonstrate that you can analyse facts and figures, prioritise information and make good decisions under pressure.

Self-Marketing Tips

Tips for tackling an in-tray exercise

- Read the instructions carefully and thoroughly.
- Try to stay calm. Keep a note of the time to ensure you pace yourself correctly.
- Read any background information you are given about the organisation, the staff and your role. Focus on key points and make brief notes.
- Scan through all items in the in-tray or email inbox to get an overall view of everything that will need to be considered.
- Prioritise according to what is most important and most urgent. Decide what can be delegated, forwarded or deferred.
- Identify key issues and any action that must be taken - detailing how, by whom and any timescales or deadlines.
- Highlight any possible resource restraints, conflicts between tasks, or implications for the organisation.
- If asked to draft a written response to any item, identify the main points of your response quickly and expand concisely on these. Keep it as brief as possible - it is easy to get absorbed in this task but be wary of time.
- Remember: there is often no right or wrong answer. Demonstrate that you have identified key issues and give your reasons for all the decisions you make.
- Work as quickly and as accurately as you can.

Self-Marketing Tips

“In a commercial environment there is less direct supervision than a graduate would have experienced at school or university. In the work place they will be expected to manage their own time efficiently, have the ability to prioritise tasks, and to be able to adapt when those priorities change.”

Anthony Hudson, Senior Manager ISCA (via GO Wales)

CHAPTER 6

Information Technology

Step 1

Review

What is Information Technology?

The increasing use of technology in all aspects of society and particularly in the workplace makes confident, creative and productive use of information technology (IT) an essential skill for life. Your IT capability encompasses not only your mastery of technical skills and techniques, but also your understanding of how to apply these skills purposefully, safely and responsibly in the workplace.

Broadly speaking, IT can be used to find, develop, analyse and present information, as well as to model situations and solve problems. IT enables rapid access to ideas and experiences from a wide range of people, communities and cultures, and allows businesses to collaborate and exchange information on a world-wide scale.

What are the Key IT Skills?

A confident IT user in the workplace is typically expected to be able to:

1. use technology to solve increasingly demanding problems and handle more complex information from a wide range of sources
2. use a range of IT tools to meet the needs of the business (maybe specific to function) and solve problems
3. develop an understanding of the need to:
   - employ safe working practices in order to minimise physical stress
   - keep business information secure and minimise risks from computer viruses and other malicious practice
   - manage information, storage and access to secure content and enable efficient retrieval
4. appreciate the impact of IT on individuals, groups and other stakeholders in the workplace by considering the social, economic, legal and ethical implications.

>>

Within business you may be expected to use a wide range of hardware and software, some of which may be industry or even business specific. However, there are a number of general IT areas with which you should feel confident when seeking to enter the workplace.

- Using the computer and accessing files
- Word Processing
- Spreadsheets
- Using databases
- Presentations
- Web browsing and communications

There may also be more specialised areas that you could consider developing your skills in depending on your career area of interest such as:

- Computer Aided Design
- Image Editing
- Health Information Systems Usage
- Project Planning
- Enterprise Resource Planning
- IT Security.

We will take some time now to ensure you are familiar with the key skills that fall within the 'general' list above.

Using the Computer and Accessing Files

To be considered employable in this area you would typically be expected to be able to demonstrate knowledge and competence in using the common functions of a personal computer and its operating system.

>>

You should be able to:

- use the main features of the operating system including adjusting the main computer settings and using built-in help features
- operate effectively around the computer desktop and work effectively in a graphical user environment
- know about the main concepts of file management and be able to efficiently organise files and folders so that they are easy to identify and find
- use utility software to compress and extract large files and use anti-virus software to protect against computer viruses
- demonstrate the ability to use simple text editing and print tools available within the operating system.

Word Processing

To be considered employable in this area you would typically be expected to be able to demonstrate the ability to use a word processing application to accomplish everyday tasks associated with creating, formatting and finishing small-sized word processing documents such as letters and other everyday documents.

You should also be able to duplicate and move text within and between documents. As a more advanced user you may be confident in creating standard tables, using pictures and images within a document, and using mail merge tools.

As a competent user of word processing software you should be able to:

- work with documents and save them in different file formats
- choose built-in options such as the Help function to enhance productivity
- create and edit small-sized word processing documents that will be ready to share and distribute
- apply different formats to documents to enhance them before distribution and recognise good practice in choosing the appropriate formatting options

>>

«

- insert tables, images and drawn objects into documents
- prepare documents for mail merge operations
- adjust document page settings and check and correct spelling before finally printing documents.

Spreadsheets

To be considered employable in this area you would typically be expected to understand the concept of spreadsheets and to be able to demonstrate the ability to use a spreadsheet application. You may also be required to accomplish tasks associated with developing, formatting, modifying and using a spreadsheet, in addition to using standard formulas and functions, and demonstrate competence in creating and formatting graphs or charts.

As a competent user of spreadsheet software you should be able to:

- work with spreadsheets and save them in different file formats
- choose built-in options such as the Help function within the application to enhance productivity
- enter data into cells and use good practice in creating lists. Select, sort and copy, move and delete data
- edit rows and columns in a worksheet. Copy, move, delete and appropriately rename worksheets
- create mathematical and logical formulas using standard spreadsheet functions. Use good practice in formula creation and recognise error values in formulas
- format numbers and text content in a spreadsheet
- choose, create and format charts to communicate information meaningfully
- adjust spreadsheet page settings and check and correct spreadsheet content before finally printing spreadsheets.

»

<<

Using Databases

To be considered employable in this area you would typically be expected to understand some of the main concepts of databases and demonstrate the ability to use a database application. This might include creating and modifying tables, queries, forms and reports, and preparing outputs ready for distribution, as well as learning to relate tables and to retrieve and manipulate information from a database by using query and sort tools.

As a competent user of database software you should be able to:

- understand what a database is and how it is organised and operated
- create a simple database and view the database content in various modes
- create a table, define and modify fields and their properties; enter and edit data in a table
- sort and filter a table or form; create, modify and run queries to retrieve specific information from a database
- understand what a form is and create a form to enter, modify and delete records and data in records
- create routine reports and prepare outputs ready for distribution.

Presentations

To be considered employable in this area you would typically be expected to demonstrate competence in using presentation tools on a computer. You should be able to accomplish tasks such as creating, formatting, modifying and preparing presentations using different slide layouts for display and printed distribution.

As a competent user of presentation software you should be able to:

- work with presentations and save them in different file formats
- choose built-in options such as the Help function within the application to enhance productivity

>>

- understand different presentation views and when to use them, choose different slide layouts and designs
- enter, edit and format text in presentations. Recognise good practice in applying unique titles to slides
- choose, create and format charts to communicate information meaningfully
- insert and edit pictures, images and drawn objects
- apply animation and transition effects to presentations and check and correct presentation content before finally printing and giving presentations.

Web Browsing and Communications

To be considered employable in this area you would typically be expected to understand some of the concepts and terms associated with using the internet, and to appreciate some of the security considerations. You would also be expected to understand some of the concepts of electronic mail (email), and demonstrate the ability to use email software to send and receive messages, and to attach files to mail messages.

As a competent user in this area you should be able to:

- understand what the internet is and common terms associated with it. Be aware of some security considerations when using the Internet
- accomplish everyday web browsing tasks including changing browser settings
- search for information and complete and submit web-based forms
- save web pages and download files from the web. Copy web content into a document
- understand what email is and know some advantages and disadvantages of its use. Be aware of other communication options
- be aware of network etiquette and security considerations when using email

>>

- create, spell check and send email. Reply to and forward email, handle file attachments and print an email
- be aware of ways to enhance productivity when working with email software. Organise and manage email.

Step 2

Assess

Carrying out an assessment of your IT skills in a guide such as this is of course impossible but it would be useful for you to take this opportunity to review your skills against the requirements listed in Step 1 and highlight any areas for improvement.

Use the table below to do so. Rate your skill level (high, medium or low) against each skill by inserting a tick in the appropriate box.

Skill	High	Medium	Low
Using the computer and accessing files			
Use the main features of the operating system including adjusting the main computer settings and using built-in help features			
Operate effectively around the computer desktop and work effectively in a graphical user environment			
Know about the main concepts of file management and be able to efficiently organise files and folders so that they are easy to identify and find			
Use utility software to compress and extract large files and use anti-virus software to protect against computer viruses			

>>

<<

Skill	High	Medium	Low
Demonstrate the ability to use simple text editing and print tools available within the operating system			
Word processing			
Work with documents and save them in different file formats			
Choose built-in options such as the Help function to enhance productivity			
Create and edit small-sized word processing documents that will be ready to share and distribute			
Apply different formats to documents to enhance them before distribution and recognise good practice in choosing the appropriate formatting options			
Insert tables, images and drawn objects into documents			
Prepare documents for mail merge operations			
Adjust document page settings and check and correct spelling before finally printing documents			
Spreadsheets			
Work with spreadsheets and save them in different file formats			
Choose built-in options such as the Help function within the application to enhance productivity			
Enter data into cells and use good practice in creating lists. Select, sort and copy, move and delete data			

>>

<<

Skill	High	Medium	Low
Edit rows and columns in a worksheet. Copy, move, delete and appropriately rename worksheets			
Create mathematical and logical formulas using standard spreadsheet functions. Use good practice in formula creation and recognise error values in formulas			
Format numbers and text content in a spreadsheet			
Choose, create and format charts to communicate information meaningfully			
Adjust spreadsheet page settings and check and correct spreadsheet content before finally printing spreadsheets			
Databases			
Understand what a database is and how it is organised and operated			
Create a simple database and view the database content in various modes			
Create a table, define and modify fields and their properties; enter and edit data in a table			
Sort and filter a table or form; create, modify and run queries to retrieve specific information from a database			
Understand what a form is and create a form to enter, modify and delete records and data in records			
Create routine reports and prepare outputs ready for distribution			

>>

<<

Skill	High	Medium	Low
Presentations			
Work with presentations and save them in different file formats			
Choose built-in options such as the Help function within the application to enhance productivity Understand different presentation views and when to use them, choose different slide layouts and designs			
Enter, edit and format text in presentations. Recognise good practice in applying unique titles to slides			
Choose, create and format charts to communicate information meaningfully			
Insert and edit pictures, images and drawn objects			
Apply animation and transition effects to presentations and check and correct presentation content before finally printing and giving presentations			
Web browsing and communications			
Understand what the internet is and common terms associated with it. Be aware of some security considerations when using the internet			
Accomplish everyday web browsing tasks including changing browser settings			
Search for information and complete and submit web-based forms			

>>

<<

Skill	High	Medium	Low
Save web pages and download files from the web. Copy web content into a document			
Understand what email is and know some advantages and disadvantages of its use. Be aware of other communication options			
Be aware of network etiquette and security considerations when using email			
Create, spell check and send email. Reply to and forward email, handle file attachments and print an email			
Be aware of ways to enhance productivity when working with email software. Organise and manage email			

Now list below the skills where you have rated yourself as low:

In your Check List (Step 6) you will need to identify ways in which these skills can be developed.

Step 3

Application (how might skill be applied)

Research suggests that skilled employees enable organisations to use technology more effectively, leading to increases in productivity and competitiveness and ensuring that operational objectives are achieved more efficiently. Moreover, digitally literate employees will also communicate more effectively both internally and externally to the clients and stakeholders of an organisation.

An IT-skilled workforce is considered to improve the efficiency and boost the productivity of individual organisations, which in turn acts as a driver for growth in the economy as a whole. A 2010 study suggests how IT-trained employees are more efficient, work more quickly, and make fewer mistakes; and the time that supervisors and other colleagues spend dealing with difficulties is halved where employees have been trained. Companies also benefit by having more accurate knowledge about the skill levels of employees and can therefore deploy them more effectively.

Digitally literate employees add real value to an organisation

- Overall efficiency and productivity is increased.
- Specific goals and objectives are more effectively achieved.
- Unnecessary administrative burdens are reduced or eliminated.
- Internal and external communication within an organisation is significantly enhanced.
- A greater uptake and utilisation of technology, resulting in greater returns on investment in that technology is ensured.
- Employees' confidence and job satisfaction are increased.
- Unnecessary time and money wasted through incompetence is eliminated.

Digitally literate employees

- Produce professional quality documents and presentations efficiently without support from other staff.

>>

<<

- Actually know the functions of their applications and use them to carry out tasks in seconds.
- Use formulas and functions to efficiently and effectively carry out complex calculations.
- Install devices independently, set them up and get on with their jobs.
- Use mail merge in word processing to get the job done in a short amount of time.
- Confidently run queries and generate reports displaying information that would take longer to produce manually.
- Manage emails effectively, understand associated risks and keep the organisation's systems secure.

Digitally illiterate employees

- Spend time trying to find and use a function that they 'know' the application can carry out.
- Waste time typing individual letters, envelope labels and other communications targeted at large groups.
- Spend a lot of time producing poor quality documents and presentations, which often need revision.
- Manually input calculable data into spreadsheets increasing the risk of errors.
- Phone helpdesk/tech support to install and set up devices and drivers and lose productivity whilst waiting for assistance.
- Struggle with databases and are 'afraid' of the application.
- Have difficulty managing their emails and are unaware of associated security risks.

Step 4

Reflect (what have I learned?)

STOP!

By now you are likely to have gained a considerable amount of information that has enabled you to reflect on your IT skills.

Task 1

Reflect on the exercise in Step 2 and write a paragraph (or two!) describing the experience below.

What areas of IT expertise do you already possess that could be attractive to a prospective employer (where did you score most highly)?

How could you demonstrate this in a job application?

«

How do you feel about your IT skills?

Task 2

How do you feel about your ability to use IT in the workplace?

Task 3

Re-read your answers to Tasks 1 and 2 above. Does anything you've written surprise you?

»

Now you've nearly reached the end of this chapter, what do you think you've learnt about this area and yourself with regard to IT in the workplace?

If you are finding this difficult, imagine that you are commenting on someone else's answers to the Task 1 and 2 questions. What would you advise them about their IT skills?

Step 5

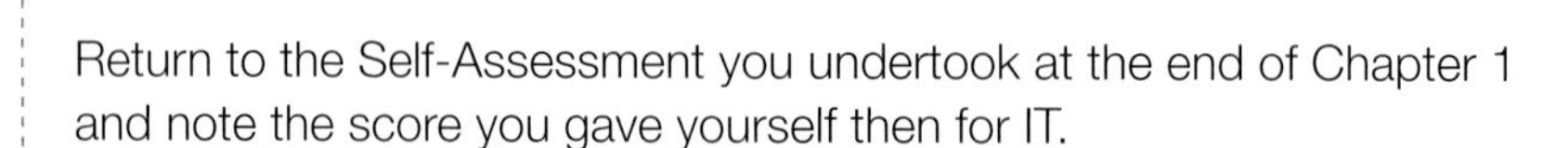

Evaluate (reach a judgement on personal performance)

So the time has come. How do you judge/rate/score your IT skills? Use the information from this chapter and the previous steps to inform your decision.

Score yourself using a scale of 0 – 10 where 0 = No Skills and 10 = Highly Skilled.

Score:

Return to the Self-Assessment you undertook at the end of Chapter 1 and note the score you gave yourself then for IT.

Self-Assessment Score:

Step 6

Check List (what next...future development)

Skill: Information Technology

Area for Improvement	I need to.....	Sources of Support	Deadline
e.g. Databases	..learn how to use databases effectively.	One of my housemates is a BIG IT user – wonder if he could teach me?.	Insert Date

Self-Marketing Tips

Given that the vast majority of job applications or speculative approaches nowadays require some engagement with information technology, there is already an expectation from your potential employer that you have a degree of IT literacy.

In fact you could almost say that the application process itself is a form of assessment of your IT skills!

However, if you have been asked to prepare documents such as a CV/Resume, covering letter or even a presentation for the interview stage this is an opportunity to really demonstrate your advanced IT skills. Equally if you are preparing a portfolio to share with the recruitment team this is another opportunity to demonstrate your IT abilities.

If you do not feel confident to prepare and present these documents in a professional manner then spend some time familiarising yourself with the style and format required (there's huge amounts of helpful material online or visit your local careers service) and then reflect on whether you currently have the IT skills to achieve this.

If you don't and it is a time sensitive issue (e.g. the application is due tomorrow), consider using a trusted friend or colleague to help you with their preparation or maybe consider paying for some expert assistance to achieve the look and feel you know will set you apart in the recruitment process.

Ultimately though you should be planning to develop the skills yourself to be able to use IT to prepare these kind of documents on an ongoing basis.

Also bear in mind that even if you have the skills yourself to prepare these materials, make sure you don't let yourself down by:

Self-Marketing Tips

1. submitting hard copies where it's clear your printer ink was running out
2. submitting hard copies on anything less than pristine, good quality paper
3. submitting hard copies where the paper wasn't aligned or the page format is not consistent with the paper size (e.g. A4 printed on letter sized paper)
4. submitting electronic copies from an email address which is less than professional (it maybe time to get a new one that doesn't include your pet name!!)
5. leaving it until the last minute to submit something online and realising your files are too big to upload!

CHAPTER 7
Communication

Step 1

Review

What is Communication?

In its purest sense communication is about a message being communicated between a 'sender' and a 'receiver'. The form of the message and its method of delivery may change and the individuals or groups involved too. Some communication is also a lot more straightforward than others in that the correct form, method, sender and receiver are involved and there is little if any interference but this is not always the case and certainly not in complex environments like businesses.

That is possibly why the Association of Graduate Recruiters suggests that 64% of employers they surveyed saw 'communication skills' as the most important skill required of their new recruits.

Communication itself covers such a broad area including spoken and written communication and all the forms that lie within just those two categories but it also extends to non-verbal communication such as body language.

In this chapter we will consider all three categories and seek to highlight some of the top tips in becoming an effective communicator!

1. Spoken Communication

Effective spoken communication requires being able to express your ideas and views clearly, confidently and concisely in speech, tailoring your content and style to the audience and promoting free-flowing communication.

- **Be clear and concise**. Vary your tone, pace and volume to enhance the communication and encourage questions.
- **Persuade and negotiate**. Arrive at an agreement that is agreeable to both sides: a win:win situation. Back up your points with logic. Show tact to those you disagree with.

- **Public presentations**. Present your message in an interesting way, structuring your presentation, using audio-visual aids effectively and building a rapport with your audience.
- **Communicate** effectively in a **team setting**.
- **Ask for help** when you need it. Research suggests that asking for help with something (within reason) makes you more liked by the person you ask!

The purpose of communication is almost limitless but if you are confirming or clarifying something you may want to consider the following advice.

- Ask yourself exactly what you want to gain from the conversation: a lack of clarity can lead to confusion and poor decisions.
- Asking clarifying questions: "How?", "Why?", "When?", "Who?", "What?", "Where?", will help the other person crystallise their thoughts.
- Summarise the main points in simple language.
- Get the other person's agreement that your summary is accurate.
- Define the problem and then move the focus to the solution: separate the points that relate to the problem and those that relate to the solution.
- Agree on the action you will both take: even if this is that there will be no action.

One of the most common forms of 'interference' or barriers to effective communication is the use of jargon, particularly within business where you can have both industry and organisation specific jargon to contend with.

So, try to:

use simple words and clear unambiguous language

be succinct: take time and effort to distil ideas to an absolute minimum

make simple points that everyone agrees on

use the active not passive voice. *"I will send it to you"* rather than *"It will be sent to you"*

avoid jargon!

>>

One of the most common forms of jargon is actually people's job titles. For example, what do you think an 'Ambient Replenishment Controller' actually does?

They stack shelves!!

The following describe some common characteristics of effective spoken conversations.

- **Make sure they are two way** with both parties equally involved and interested. It is a shared experience. It is a partnership like a dance: you respond to each other's movements and are both winners.
- **Build them around respect:** treat other people the way you want to be treated yourself. The atmosphere should feel comfortable: like plants, conversations need good ground to take root and flourish.
- **Talk about mainly positive things**. People who talk about good news tend to cheer people up whereas people who always talk in negatives tend to depress the people they are talking to! Obviously there must be a balance, as sometimes we must talk about unhappy events, but make sure you don't do this too much.
- There should be a **willingness to be open** on both sides. Each person has the opportunity to express their point of view and feelings. Relationships develop through conversations where we open up and exchange details to create closeness.
- Always **address someone by their first name** if you know this. It shows that you are treating them as an individual.
- A good conversation **makes a difference**; something useful happens and it has a satisfying conclusion.
- **Nod your head** from time to time to encourage the speaker.
- **Leave spaces**: stay silent for a few seconds. Don't talk for too long: our attention only lasts a few minutes before we need a break. Cut your story into bite-sized chunks to allow breathing space.
- **Make descriptions specific**: don't generalise or use clichés. Be precise and concrete.
- **Ask the speaker to elaborate** on major points.

<<

- **Regularly summarising** can improve the quality and accuracy of your conversations. Feed brief summaries back into the conversation.
- **When starting conversations** show that you value the other person's attention: "I'd really like your opinion about ....."

2. Written Communication

The Recruitment and Employment Commission (REC) states that around half of all CVs received by recruitment consultants contain spelling or grammatical errors. THAT IS A SHOCKING STATISTIC!

Candidates aged between 21 and 25 are most likely to make these mistakes and graduates in this age group are, surprisingly, twice as likely to make mistakes as those who did not go on to university. Even something as basic as the name of an employer, or an individual recruiter, is often spelled incorrectly.

Written Communication involves expressing yourself clearly, using language with precision; constructing a logical argument; note taking, editing and summarising; and writing reports.

There are three main elements to written communication.

- **Structure** (the way the content is laid out).
- **Style** (the way it is written).
- **Content** (what you are writing about).

Structure and layout can be relatively quickly learnt but learning how to write good quality content takes much longer.

A checklist for this, against which you can assess your own writing follows below.

Structure (the way the content is laid out)

- Is the layout clear and easy to follow?
- Do headings stand out (e.g. are they in a larger font size)?
- Is the information arranged in a logical sequence with a beginning (introduction), middle and end (conclusion)?

>>

<<

- Does the introduction clearly state the subject and purpose?
- Does it briefly summarise the content?

Style (the way it is written)

- Does it look neat, and elegant?
- Is it concise, with an exact use of words and economy of style? For example, instead of saying forward planning, just say planning - there is no such thing as backward planning!
- Is it simple, direct and lucid?
- Are paragraphs too long? Paragraphs of less than 10 lines are easier to read.
- Is a blank line left between paragraphs to aid clarity?
- Are sentences too long? A sentence should contain just one idea.
- Sentences with more than 30 words should normally be split.
- Is the first sentence interesting? Does it draw the reader in?
- Have you avoided unnecessary jargon?
- Is the style suitable for the intended audience? Are bulleted lists used where appropriate?
- Have you used short, concrete, familiar words rather than long, obscure, complex words?
- Have you used active words where possible rather than the passive voice? *"It is recommended ...."* should be replaced by *"We recommend"* as this is simpler and more direct
- Have you kept wordy phrases to a minimum?
- Have you avoided repetition?
- The Campaign for Plain English recommends sans serif fonts (e.g. Arial, Verdana) such as this, as clearer and easier to read than serif fonts (e.g. Times New Roman, Garamond) such as this.

>>

Content (what you are writing about)

- Have you carefully checked the spelling and punctuation (avoid 'text speak' at all costs – the most common mistake with this is writing 'no' instead of 'know'!!)?
- Have you thought through in advance what you want to say?
- Have you a clear objective?
- Have you listed the essential points you wish to make?
- Have you made these points clearly?
- Have you developed your argument in a logical way?
- Have you allowed detail to obscure the main issues?
- Is the content positive and constructive?
- Have you shown an interest in the reader by writing with warmth, sensitivity and friendliness?
- Have you edited it through several revisions, honing the text until it is just right?
- Have you left it overnight if possible: your mind will assimilate it better and you will come back with a fresh view.

3. Non-Verbal Communication

Research has suggested that as much as 55% of what we communicate is communicated by us non-verbally: by our body language. This is particularly relevant in high stress situations such as recruitment where we are trying to present ourselves in the most positive light but our body language betrays how anxious and nervous we really are!

Keep the following tips in mind to try and address this.

- **Smile!**
- Be prepared to **shake hands firmly**, but don't break the interviewer's wrist. Similarly a "wet fish" (weak) handshake will suggest a weak character.

>>

- **Wait** to be invited to sit down.
- Try to **relax** - don't sit on the edge of your chair and don't lean too far back: sit up reasonably straight and still.
- **Don't sit with your arms crossed** as this is considered to be a defensive posture and acts like a barrier between you and the other person.
- Keep up **good eye contact** with the interviewer but don't make it too intense, aim to break the connection every 30-40 seconds.
- **Speak clearly but not too fast:** a deeper calm voice suggests authority, whereas an excitable high-pitched voice suggests a nervous personality.
- **Head nodding** to show agreement can help, but don't overdo your enthusiasm!
- **Postural echo** (mirroring the interviewer's posture) can show empathy and agreement but needs to be done **very subtly** or it might backfire if the interviewer notices that you are doing this!

Step 2

Assess

Communication

Use the following diagnostic tool to assess your skills in these areas.

Rate the frequency of your actions against each statement by inserting a tick in the appropriate box.

	Not at all	Rarely	Sometimes	Often	Very Often
I try to anticipate and predict possible causes of confusion, and I deal with them up front.					
When I write a memo, email, or other document, I give all of the background information and detail I can to make sure that my message is understood.					
If I don't understand something, I tend to keep this to myself and figure it out later.					
I'm sometimes surprised to find that people haven't understood what I've said.					
I can tend to say what I think, without worrying about how the other person perceives it. I assume that we'll be able to work it out later.					
When people talk to me, I try to see their perspectives.					

>>

	Not at all	Rarely	Sometimes	Often	Very Often
I use email to communicate complex issues with people. It's quick and efficient.					
When I finish writing a report, memo, or email, I scan it quickly for typos and so forth, and then send it off right away.					
When talking to people, I pay attention to their body language.					
I use diagrams and charts to help express my ideas.					
Before I communicate, I think about what the person needs to know, and how best to convey it.					
When someone's talking to me, I think about what I'm going to say next to make sure I get my point across correctly.					
Before I send a message, I think about the best way to communicate it (in person, over the phone, in a newsletter, via memo, and so on).					
I try to help people understand the underlying concepts behind the point I am discussing. This reduces misconceptions and increases understanding.					
I consider cultural barriers when planning my communications.					

Now use the following key to score your responses.

Not at all	Rarely	Sometimes	Often	Very Often
1	2	3	4	5
1	2	3	4	5
5	4	3	2	1
5	4	3	2	1
5	4	3	2	1
1	2	3	4	5
5	4	3	2	1
5	4	3	2	1
1	2	3	4	5
1	2	3	4	5
1	2	3	4	5
1	2	3	4	5
1	2	3	4	5
1	2	3	4	5
1	2	3	4	5

My total score is ....

Score 56 – 75

Excellent! You understand your role as a communicator, both when you send messages, and when you receive them. You anticipate problems, and you choose the right ways of communicating. People respect you for your ability to communicate clearly, and they appreciate your listening skills.

Score 36 – 55

You're a capable communicator, but you sometimes experience communication problems. Take the time to think about your approach to communication, and focus on receiving messages effectively, as much as sending them. This will help you improve.

Score 15 – 35

You need to keep developing your communication skills. You are not always expressing yourself clearly, and you may not be receiving messages correctly either. The good news is that, by paying attention to communication, you can be much more effective at work, and enjoy much better working relationships!

Step 3

Application (how might skill be applied)

According to The Times 100, Bernard Matthews is the largest turkey producer in the UK. The business has grown significantly since it began in 1950, when Bernard Matthews bought 20 turkey eggs and a second-hand incubator. Twelve turkeys successfully hatched from this initial batch and before long, the young entrepreneur was able to give up his insurance job and concentrate full-time on rearing turkeys.

Today, Bernard Matthews rears over seven million turkeys every year. 13 million UK households buy a Bernard Matthews Farms branded product each year. Despite the size of its operations, the company remains close to its roots in East Anglia with its farms located across Norfolk, Suffolk and Lincolnshire. Bernard Matthews operates in a competitive and fast-changing environment. Consumers are faced with a huge choice of foods to suit different lifestyles, diets and tastes. However, in recent years, buying patterns have changed as consumers have become more concerned about healthy eating, food safety and animal welfare.

Fast-changing environment

Chance events can have a significant impact on a food business. For example, Jamie Oliver's high-profile campaign in 2005 to improve the quality of school meals singled out foods such as Bernard Matthews' Turkey Twizzlers as being unhealthy. In 2007, there was an outbreak of bird flu at a Bernard Matthews farm in Suffolk. At this time, the media also discovered that the company imported some of its turkey from abroad. The press published stories that this could have been directly related to the outbreak, a theory that was never proved.

Initially, Bernard Matthews did not speak up and defend its product range, which offered affordable, tasty and convenient food for everyday working families. This resulted in adverse press coverage and the company lost credibility with the media. When bird flu hit relations with the media were at an all-time low. The company's immediate reaction to the crisis was to focus on eliminating the disease, which it did successfully.

Communications came low on the list of priorities. This meant that the resulting information 'vacuum' was soon filled with damaging and often inaccurate news reports.

>>

When the company realised the extent of the damage and finally opened up to the press it was too little, too late, as all trust had been lost. As a result, Bernard Matthews' sales in the UK fell by 35% and the company went into a loss position.

In 2008, the company implemented a business turnaround programme. From a communications perspective this involved:

- more closely monitoring the changing environment in which the company operates
- understanding the customer's needs better
- communicating in a transparent manner with all stakeholders to rebuild trust in the company.

In 2010 Bernard Matthews reported profits had risen to 2.5million GBP.

Communicating effectively at the individual, group, business or industry level is crucial to business success.

> "Written communications skills are more important than ever. Most of the communication that takes place within our company, and with our customers, is conducted electronically. It is therefore a fundamental requirement of our employees to be able to express themselves clearly and concisely, and to be able to adapt their style of writing according to the intended audience."

Anthony Hudson, Senior Manager at ICSA (via GO Wales)

Step 4

Reflect (what have I learned?)

STOP!

By now you are likely to have gained a considerable amount of information that has enabled you to reflect on your communication skills.

Task 1

Reflect on the exercise in Step 2 and write a paragraph (or two!) describing the experience below.

Are you more effective as a written or spoken communicator? If so, why do you think this is the case?

What feedback have you received previously about your communication skills?

>>

How do you feel about your communication skills?

Task 2

How do you feel about your ability to communicate effectively in the workplace?

<<

Task 3

Re-read your answers to Tasks 1 and 2 above. Does anything you've written surprise you?

Now you've nearly reached the end of this chapter, what do you think you've learnt about this area and yourself with regard to communication skills in the workplace?

If you are finding this difficult, imagine that you are commenting on someone else's answers to the Task 1 and 2 questions. What would you advise them about their communication skills?

Step 5

Evaluate (reach a judgement on personal performance)

So the time has come. How do you judge/rate/score your communication skills? Use the information from this chapter and the previous steps to inform your decision.

Score yourself using a scale of 0 – 10 where 0 = No Skills and 10 = Highly Skilled.

Score:

Return to the Self-Assessment you undertook at the end of Chapter 1 and note the score you gave yourself then for communication.

Self-Assessment Score:

Step 6

Check List (what next...future development)

Skill: Communication

Area for Improvement	**I need to.....**	**Sources of Support**	**Deadline**
e.g. Non-verbal communication	..stop folding my arms in an interview setting.	Practise my interview technique with a careers advisor and ask for feedback on this.	Insert Date

Self marketing is all about communication: how you communicate your personal brand.

"My tip – Above all, do/achieve something! Record your achievements and be prepared to talk about them. Share your passion."

Daniel Merriott, Consultant (via Twitter)
www.danielmerriott.net

First you need to be clear about that personal brand.

Who are you?
What are the strengths that you want to share?
What do you want to achieve?
What makes you different from others?

Then you need to decide how best to communicate this.

It should be clearly communicated through ALL of your written and spoken communication (and your non-verbal too!).

For example, Jim is about to finish his degree in design and is seeking to secure a position with a design agency that specialises in product design for the small electronics industry.

Jim has been intent on this career since his GCSEs and has been working on his design portfolio ever since. For his A level coursework he analysed the product design of several high profile small electronic firms and he sought out some work shadowing experience with a local design agency, which, although it wasn't product

Self Marketing Tips

related, it gave him an insight into the commercial design process.

All of this he used as evidence when applying to Universities and colleges and since starting his degree he has continued to grow his portfolio of evidence ready for the time when he would begin job seeking.

During this period Jim has become particularly interested in audio speaker design and entered a Young Entrepreneur's competition with a design of his own. He didn't win the competition but has used the feedback from the judges to enhance his prototype further.

Jim's brand is starting to emerge…he is a young, creative strategic thinker who is objective driven. The key strength, upon which he has received most positive feedback, is his ability to formulate and implement a plan to achieve his goals. His goal, as previously stated, is to secure a position in the design industry and what makes him different is that he's already started networking within the industry. After the competition he entered received national press coverage he sent a copy of the press article with a speculative letter to six design agencies that he had targeted. Four didn't even bother to reply but one is owned by a designer who welcomed Jim's well-planned approach and has already offered him an interview once his degree is complete.

CHAPTER 8
Teamworking

Step 1

Review

What is Teamworking?

“Teamworking may be defined as a work practice based on the use of teams, or groups of limited numbers of people, who have shared objectives at work and who co-operate, on a permanent or temporary basis, to achieve those objectives in a way that allows each individual to make a distinctive contribution.”

CIPD[1]

So let's take a moment to consider some of the key elements of that definition:

- shared objectives
- co-operation
- individual contribution.

There are three distinct skill sets arising here:

- objective setting
- cooperation
- making an individual contribution.

So to be effective at teamworking we must be skilled in each of these areas.

1 CIPD Fact Sheet (March 2011) Available from http://www.cipd.co.uk/hr-resources/factsheets/teamworking.aspx#link_0

"Regardless of the size of company, the ability to work as part of a team is critical. An employee can only be effective at his job if he is able to co-operate with other people, both within his own department and across the company as a whole."

Anthony Hudson, Senior Manager ISCA (via Go Wales)

1. Objective Setting

In business terms, an objective is commonly defined as an end that can be reasonably achieved within an expected timeframe and with available resources. In general, an objective is broader in scope than a goal, and may consist of several individual goals. Objectives are basic tools that underly all planning and strategic activities.

Setting objectives then requires the ability to plan effectively; to identify the tasks required to meet the objective, calculate the time the tasks will take and what resources will be required to carry them out.

Objective setting also requires an ability to see the 'bigger picture'; to be aware of how each objective contributes to the bigger objective it may form part of.

For example, Company A has a corporate objective to increase its sales by 10% in the next year of trading. Individual departments within that company will set their own objectives to ensure they contribute to that overall corporate objective. The marketing department may set an objective to increase awareness of the company's products amongst a new market segment in order to achieve the increase in sales. The production department may set an objective to improve the efficiency of the production line by 4% in order to be able to fulfil the additional orders that this increase in sales will bring.

It would be no good if the production department set an objective to reduce capacity in some way when the organisation actually required them to meet the additional new orders coming in!!

>>

<<

Take Action!

Spend a couple of minutes thinking of one of your own personal objectives and note it below.

e.g. I want to find a junior management position in Mechanical Engineering when I finish my degree.

Now take a look at that objective and identify a number of 'smaller' objectives that you might set in order to achieve the main objective.

e.g. Complete my degree, achieving the minimum of a 2:1 classification.

e.g. Identify a range of organisations to which I can make speculative job applications.

Next, what tasks would be required to achieve your 'smaller objectives'?

How much time would these take?

What resources would be required?

>>

SMART Objectives

SMART is a mnemonic commonly used to ensure that objectives set are well constructed.

Letter	Major Term	Minor Terms
S	Specific	Significant, Stretching, Simple
M	Measurable	Meaningful, Motivational, Manageable
A	Attainable	Appropriate, Achievable, Agreed, Assignable, Actionable, Ambitious, Aligned, Aspirational
R	Relevant	Realistic, Resourced, Resonant
T	Time-bound	Time-oriented, Time framed, Timed, Time-based, Timeboxed, Timely, Time-Specific, Timetabled, Time limited, Trackable, Tangible

The objective should be 'assessed' against the criteria set by the mnemonic.

For example, if we return to the earlier objective:

I want to find a junior management position in Mechanical Engineering when I finish my degree.

How specific is this objective? Could we make it any more specific?

Possibly we could make the junior management position more specific by adding something further such as salary expectations or number of direct reports.

I want to find a junior management position, earning a minimum of £25k, in Mechanical Engineering when I finish my degree.

How measurable is this objective? Could we make it any more measurable?

Well in fact the salary expectation has made it more measurable also.

How attainable is this objective? Could we make it any more attainable?

Given this objective, we would have to ask if the degree for which the objective setter is studying is appropriate for a career in Mechanical Engineering? Also, if, for a graduate, a management position is achievable immediately?

>>

<<

How relevant is this objective? Could we make it any more relevant?

As a personal objective then it must be VERY relevant…unless there is some external influence that is 'shaping' this? Does this person really want to work in Mechanical Engineering?

How time-bound is this objective? Could we make it any more time-bound?

Yes, the objective is not specific about time:

I want to find a junior management position, earning a minimum of £25k, in Mechanical Engineering ***when I finish my degree.***

We could easily improve this by changing it to:

I want to find a junior management position, earning a minimum of £25k, in Mechanical Engineering ***within a year of finishing my degree.***

This also has the benefit of making the objective far more measurable.

Now take a moment or two to 'SMART'en up your own objective!

2. Co-operation

So how do we co-operate most effectively?

According to a Guardian article written by Browning, the jury is out as to whether human beings are naturally co-operative.

It may simply be the case that humans work together because the tasks they tackle are simply too big for one person.

"They say too many cooks spoil the broth, but they also say many hands make light work. The trick is having one person work on the soup and the rest on the electrics." [2]

2 Browning, G (2008) How to Cooperate. The Guardian. Available from http://www.guardian.co.uk/lifeandstyle/2008/mar/15/healthandwellbeing.features

Effective co-operation is commonly considered to include the following elements.

- Mutual Self-Interest
    - It is hugely important before you begin to work as a team to emphasise what everyone is going to gain from you all working together. Make it LOUD and CLEAR what everyone 'wins' from this experience. If you can find common ground here – even better!
- Ability to Listen
    - Listening skills themselves could take up a whole chapter but simply make sure that you are an 'active' listener when co-operating. Another mnemonic such as SOLER may help here:
        - S = Squarely face the other person
        - O = Open your posture
        - L = Lean towards the person speaking
        - E = Maintain eye contact
        - R = Relax
- 'Give and Take'/Compromise
    - Compromise is by far one of the most difficult elements of co-operation. It is useful if you have a clear idea where and when you are willing to compromise and where and when you are not! However, it is vital that you have an objective and well-supported argument related to your objectives on areas/issues you are not willing to compromise on rather than sounding like a petulant child!

3. Individual Contribution

What do you bring individually to the team? Maybe you are not sure even why you have been asked to join the team. If you are unable to answer this question then you need to find the answer. That might be from some personal reflection, it may be from simply asking the question of others in your team or the individual who appointed you.

Whichever way you find out the answer to this question – it is crucial that you understand what is required of you and the VALUE you bring to your team.

A lack of clarity on this is likely to mean that you will be an ineffectual team member.

Step 2

Assess

Use the following diagnostic tool[3] to assess your typical contribution to teamwork.

Put a tick (✔) in the box next to the statements that you think BEST reflect your behaviour whilst working in a team.

REMEMBER - The more honest your assessment here the more value you will gain from this whole process.

Statement	✔	Key
I help others to find compromises between differing viewpoints.		**C**
I introduce new ideas to groups in which I work.		**I**
I try to decide on the criteria on which I will make my decisions and then stick to these.		**E**
I am not swayed by emotional arguments.		**S**
I am an optimist who tends to look on the positive side.		**En**
I am a well-organised individual who is good at keeping to deadlines.		**R**
I build on the ideas of others.		**S**

>>

3 Adapted from the University of Kent Careers. Available from http://www.kent.ac.uk/careers/sk/teamwork.htm

Statement	✔	Key
I stick up for my opinions and try to argue persuasively and with logic for them.		**L**
I suggest new ways of doing things.		**I**
I make sure all possibilities are explored.		**S**
I act as the note-taker for the groups I am involved in.		**R**
I support and praise other team members.		**En**
I elaborate on what others have said.		**S**
I am willing to compromise my own view to obtain a group consensus.		**C**
I use humour to remove stresses in groups in which I work.		**En**
I act as the spokesperson, to deliver the findings of the group.		**R**
I clarify other people's contributions.		**S**
I am more concerned with major issues than with details.		**I**
I try hard to keep up the group's energy level.		**En**
I try to keep relations between group members harmonious.		**C**
I ask others to take responsibility for particular tasks.		**L**
I use dispassionate, critical analysis to make decisions.		**E**
I summarise what has been said.		**S**
I usually lead and co-ordinate the team effort.		**L**
I don't allow the group to over-run the time limit for the task.		**R**
I listen carefully to what the other team members have to say and try to get quiet group members to contribute.		**C**
I suggest new ways of looking at problems.		**I**

>>

<<

Now count up the number of ticks (✔) you have recorded against each of the key codes in the boxes below.

Key	No. of
En	
C	
L	
S	
I	
E	
R	

Note against which key codes you have scored most highly and identify the role(s) from the list below.

En = Encourager

C = Compromiser

L = Leader

S = Summariser/Clarifier

I = Ideas Person

E = Evaluator

R = Recorder

I score most highly as:

Encourager

They are tolerant individuals and good listeners who will listen carefully to the views of other group members. They are good judges of people, diplomatic and sensitive to the feelings of others and not seen as a threat. Able to recognise and resolve differences of opinion and the the development of conflict, they enable "difficult" team-members to contribute positively.

>>

They may say:

"We haven't heard from Mike yet: I'd like to hear what you think about this."

"I'm not sure I agree. What are your reasons for saying that?"

Compromiser

Tries to maintain harmony among the team members. They are sociable, interested in others and will enjoy introducing people, draw them out and make them feel comfortable. They may be willing to change their own views to get a group decision. They work well with different people and can be depended on to promote a positive atmosphere, helping the team to gel. They pull people and tasks together, developing rapport.

Leader

Good leaders direct the sequence of steps the group takes and keep the group "on-track". They are good at controlling people and events and coordinating resources. They have the energy, determination and initiative to overcome obstacles and bring competitive drive to the team. They give shape to the team effort. They recognise the skills of individuals and how they can be used. Leaders are outgoing individuals who have to be careful not to be domineering. They can sometimes steamroller the team but get results quickly. They may become impatient with complacency and lack of progress and may sometimes overreact.

They may say:

"Let's come back to this later if we have time."

"We need to move on to the next step."

"Sue, what do you think about this idea?"

Summariser/Clarifier

Calm, reflective individuals who summarise the group's discussion and conclusions. They clarify group objectives and elaborate on the ideas of others. They may go into detail about how the group's plans would work and tie up loose ends. They are good mediators and seek consensus.

They may say:

"So here's what we've decided so far" "I think you're right, but we could also add ...."

>>

Ideas person

The ideas person suggests new ideas to solve group problems or new ways for the group to organise the task. They dislike orthodoxy and are not too concerned with practicalities. They provide suggestions and proposals that are often original and radical. They are more concerned with the big picture than with details. May get bored after the initial impetus wears off.

They may say:

"Why don't we consider doing it this way?"

Evaluator

Evaluators help the group avoid coming to agreement too quickly. They tend to be slow in coming to a decision because of a need to think things over. They are the logical, analytical, objective people in the team and offer measured, dispassionate critical analysis. They contribute at times of crucial decision making because they are capable of evaluating competing proposals. They may suggest alternative ideas.

They may say:

"What other possibilities are there?"

"Let's try to look at this another way."

"I'm not sure we're on the right track."

Recorder

The recorder keeps the group focused and organised. They make sure that everyone is helping with the project. They are usually the first person to offer to take notes to keep a record of ideas and decisions. They also like to act as time-keeper, to allocate times to specific tasks and remind the team to keep to them, or a spokesperson, to deliver the ideas and findings of the group. They may check that all members understand and agree on plans and actions and know their roles and responsibilities. They may act as the memory of the group.

They may say:

"We only have five minutes left, so we need to come to agreement now!"

"Do we all understand this chart?"

"Are we all in agreement on this?"

Step 3

Application (how might skill be applied)

Organisations use teamworking for many reasons, including the desire to achieve the following types of objectives. To:

- improve productivity
- enhance quality of products or services
- improve customer focus
- speed the spread of ideas
- respond to opportunities and threats and to fast-changing environments
- increase employee motivation
- introduce multi-skilling and employee flexibility.

There can be benefits for employees too. The most commonly-quoted positive outcomes are greater job satisfaction and motivation together with improved learning.

<<

An effective team has the following characteristics:

- a common sense of purpose
- a clear understanding its own objectives
- resources to achieve those objectives
- mutual respect among team members, both as individuals and for the contribution each makes to the team's performance
- valuing members' strengths and respecting their weaknesses
- mutual trust
- willingness to share knowledge and expertise
- willingness to speak openly
- a range of skills among team members to deal effectively with all its tasks
- a range of personal styles for the various roles needed to carry out the team's tasks.

So if any of these elements are not present it is your responsibility to work with your fellow team members to secure them.

Reflect (what have I learned?)

STOP!

By now you are likely to have gained a considerable amount of information about teamwork and yourself as a team member both from your experiences during your studies, other work experience you may have gained and by working through this chapter. Let's take some time to make sense of it all.

>>

<<

Task 1

Pick an example of teamwork in which you've been involved and write a paragraph (or two!) describing the experience below.

Focus on the three key elements in your writing:

Objective setting
Cooperation
Individual contribution

Is this example 'typical' of your teamwork experience? If not, what makes it different?

>>

<<

Task 2

Looking back on this and other experiences of teamwork you've had, how do you feel about teamwork?

Task 3

Re-read your answers to Tasks 1 and 2 above. Does anything you've written surprise you?

Now you've nearly reached the end of this chapter, what do you think you've learnt about teamwork and yourself as a team member? If you are finding this difficult, imagine that you are commenting on someone else's answers to the Task 1 and 2 questions. What would you advise them about teamwork?

Step 5

Evaluate (reach a judgement on personal performance)

So the time has come. How do you judge/rate/score yourself at teamwork? Use the information from this chapter and the previous steps to inform your decision.

Score:

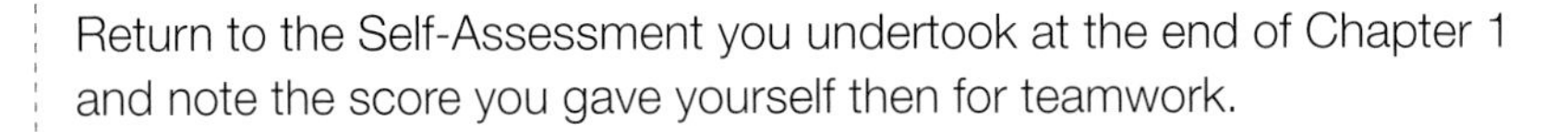

Return to the Self-Assessment you undertook at the end of Chapter 1 and note the score you gave yourself then for teamwork.

Self-Assessment Score:

Do these scores differ? If so, why do you think this might be?

Step 6

Check List (what next...future development)

Skill: Teamwork

Area for Improvement	**I need to.....**	**Sources of Support**	**Deadline**
e.g. Listening	..make more eye contact when listening.	Ask trusted friends/colleagues to give me feedback when we are talking.	Insert Date

Self-Marketing Tips

As always, if applying for an 'advertised' position it is important to thoroughly analyse the advertisement before you begin; to identify the skills that are explicitly required (some may be considered Essential and some Desirable but nevertheless they want them all!!).

So what reference to teamwork do they make in the advertisement?

In carrying out your further research about the organisation, what mention do they make of teamwork? Are there examples on their website or annual report of their teams in action? See if you can speak to one of their existing employees and ask about how they work in teams. What language do they use in talking about the value of teamwork?

By 'mirroring' the way in which the organisation uses language to discuss a skill set you are making the job of the HR person or recruiting manager that much easier when reading your application.

If you are making a speculative application to the organisation then the same approach is equally valuable. You won't have an advertisement or job description to work from but with some diligent research you can learn a great deal about the organisation's approach to and perspective on teamwork which you can then reflect in your application.

CV/Resume

Depending on the approach you've taken with your CV/Resume there are a number of ways in which you can highlight your teamwork skills.

Make reference to yourself as a team player/leader in your personal profile section (remember to mirror the language the recruiting organisation uses).

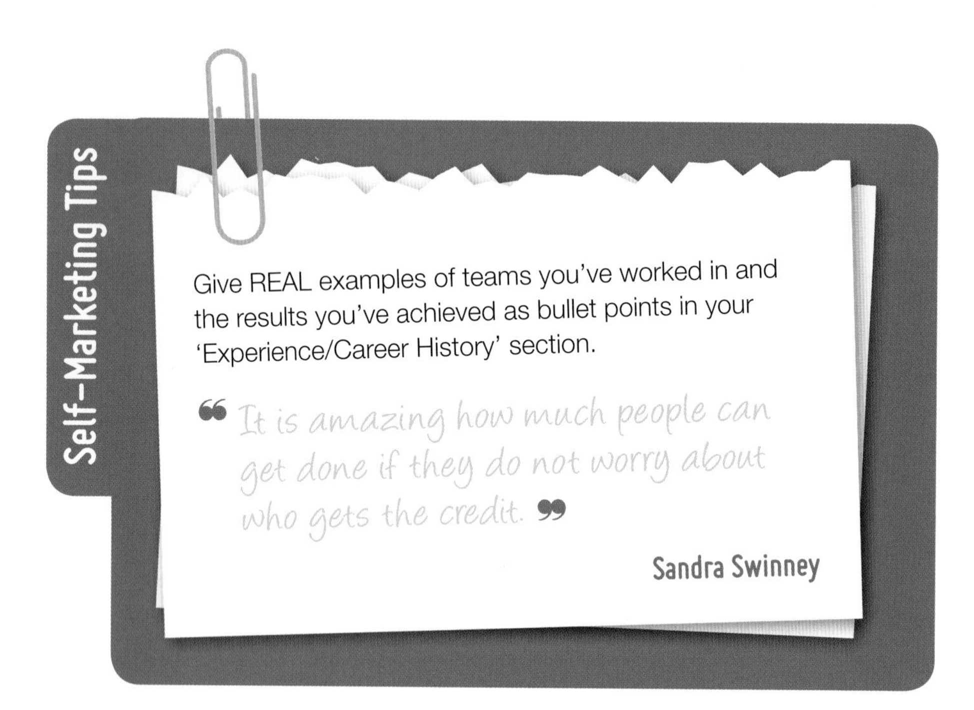
Self-Marketing Tips
Give REAL examples of teams you've worked in and the results you've achieved as bullet points in your 'Experience/Career History' section.
"It is amazing how much people can get done if they do not worry about who gets the credit."
Sandra Swinney

CHAPTER 9
Self-Management Skills

Step 1

Review

What is Self-Management?

Self-management skills are those skills that allow an employee to be more productive when doing daily routine tasks, regardless of the working environment. Well-developed self-management skills will help you efficiently communicate with co-workers, management and customers, make 'good' decisions, plan your working time, and ensure your physical well-being.

The type of skills that typically fall within this area are (although this is by no means an exhaustive list) are:

- readiness to accept responsibility
- flexibility
- resilience
- appropriate assertiveness
- time management
- readiness to improve performance based on feedback/reflective learning
- planning/organisational skills
- contingency planning
- ability to prioritise effectively
- maintaining your personal appearance
- working under pressure.

Developing self-management skills becomes one of the best management practices and activities of those people who have decided to become more productive employees. As a prospective employee, being able to demonstrate these skills or your plan to develop these skills is a particularly 'attractive offer' to any potential employer.

While companies tend to spend large amounts of both money and energy to provide their employees with special self-management skills training, it is possible for you to personally organise self-assessment surveys to define whether you already have the required skills. Step 2 below is your first attempt at this. This is extremely important if you are oriented towards career development.

Without the personal effort for developing self-organisation and self-management skills, it's hard to imagine a productive employee succeeding in career promotion and professional advancement.

Unfortunately we do not have the potential within this guide to cover all the skill sets which typically falls within this area, so we have chosen to focus on three that do not typically get a lot of 'coverage' in employability texts, namely, assertiveness, prioritising and physical presentation.

" Be as proactive as you can whilst at uni by volunteering, running societies etc as it really sets you apart & offers unique exp! "

Graduate Jobs UK (via Twitter) www.graduate-jobs.com

1. Assertiveness

Assertiveness is the ability to communicate with others in a clear and direct manner. It differs from being aggressive, where you may get what you want, but may upset people and hinder your progress in the long run.

Some people confuse assertiveness with getting your own way all the time, but there may be occasions when you take the decision to back down on an issue, because you realise that the other person has rights too. It also differs from being passive, where you let others get their own way in most situations and don't stand up for your rights.

Assertive behaviour helps you:

- say "No" to the requests of others in a firm but polite way when you don't want to do as they say
- to avoid being manipulated or put off by others

>>

<<

- to listen better to what others are saying
- to stand up for your rights
- to ask for what you want
- to achieve "win-win" situations where both parties are happy with the outcome of the situation.

Being assertive helps you to exercise more control over your life and relationships, and thus may help to increase your self-confidence. It helps you to reduce the stress in your life as you are less bothered about the opinions of others. Non-assertive behaviour can lead to loss of respect from others and loss of self-respect in the long term.

Assertive behaviour can be characterised by:

- a firm clear voice
- eye contact with the interviewer
- being relaxed rather than nervous
- an open body posture (e.g. don't have your arms and legs folded tightly)
- saying what you want to say using simple, clear language
- a direct open manner.

2. Prioritisation

Time management trainers typically suggest that good prioritisation comes down to planning. They recommend that you write down a list of what you want to do and then decide how the activities on your list fit into your overall goals.

Alternatively, divide tasks into achievable targets. Then look at day-to-day tasks and determine if they advance you towards the objective. Where does most benefit lie? Psychologists even suggest that you undertake this list making before you sleep so that your unconscious has time to solve the problems as you sleep!

However, in large organisations – and particularly if you have multiple bosses – it can still be extra difficult to identify priorities. If you're

>>

unsure, ask your customers, line managers and colleagues what they consider important. If you have a mentor, ask them.

It may also be possible to question or challenge the person – is this important for me to do? Is this a priority? It is also important that you feel able to say no. Explain that you already have things to do – ask them, 'Which task do you want me to do?'

The most common issue with an individual's ability to prioritise typically stems from a lack of planning. Assuming you have planned you must still stick to what is important: most people rightly tackle tasks that are urgent and important first. But many then make the mistake of moving on to tasks that are urgent, but not important. Stay in the 'important area'! It's also important that you don't let the technology dictate your priorities, such as your email list – simply because someone has just sent you an email doesn't mean they necessarily need an immediate reply!

3. Physical Presentation

Keeping your body in good shape is a critical self-management skill. When you feel healthy and have a robust nervous system, you can do more things and cope with many challenges. Physical activity (like jogging, fitness, different sorts of sports, etc.) allows you to strengthen your body, keep your muscles up, and be more productive.

As well as caring for your physical well-being it is also important to ensure you present yourself in an appropriate manner in the workplace. Does your potential employer have a dress code for example? If you have visited their site or seen photographs of their staff do you observe a common style of personal presentation? Even if they have a fairly relaxed dress code, there is normally an expectation that you would dress more formally for the recruitment process.

Do not panic and think you need to spend a fortune on designer gear, you simply need to ensure that:

1. your clothes are clean and in good repair
2. they are appropriate for the workplace (e.g. a shirt/blouse and a pair of dark trousers – not denim!)
3. they are 'modest' and reveal a minimum amount of skin

<<

4. you have paid attention to your personal care (e.g. your hair is washed, teeth are clean and you are not wearing chipped nail polish!)

Maintaining good physical presentation whilst in your new role is also important; do not let your standards slip as this can be construed as a lack of commitment to or interest in your new career.

Step 2

Assess

Use the following diagnostic tool to assess your time management skills.

For each of the following, choose the answer that is the best fit for your time management style. Best fit means that it is the answer that is true for the majority (but may not be all of the time).

REMEMBER - The more honest your assessment here the more value you will gain from this whole process.

1. I record new appointments, meetings or other time commitments:

a) into my planner (electronic or paper)

b) onto a wall or desk pad calendar

c) on to a sticky note or scrap of paper that i paste on my wall, mirror, computer monitor or other location i associate with this task

d) consistently in two of the above locations

e) in all of the above with no consistent pattern

2. When arriving to an appointment, I am usually:

a) 10-15 minutes early

b) right on time

c) more than 15 minutes early

d) 10-15 minutes late

e) more than 15 minutes late

>>

3. When deadlines are approaching, I:

a) don't see it as a problem as i have carefully scheduled my time and have not left everything to the last minute

b) 'feel the heat' but i am confident that i can complete it on time

c) get a bit anxious and make sure i don't have any plans on the due date so i can work overtime if needed

d) panic as i have no idea where i am at with the project

e) ask for an extension

4. When you are asked to take on an additional task you:

a) consider your other commitments and block off time or rearrange priorities to manage this new task into your calendar

b) feel stressed that you have to change your plans around to accommodate this new work

c) delegate things to someone else so that you can make room for this new task

d) resist it, consider saying no

e) refuse it as you are over worked and can't possibly fit in another task.

If your answers are mostly:

a) you are a good time manager and probably could teach others how to manage their time

b) you are a fairly good time manager with some minor areas of weakness that could be looked at

c) you manage your time but you are using approaches that don't always work out as they are risky. try to use more conventional time management techniques to improve your skills

d) take a serious look at how your time management skills are affecting your performance. read some books on time management or take a course

e) work hard to improve your skills. you may be passed over for a promotion or fail to fulfil your job role if your time management skills do not improve.

>>

Step 3

Application (how might skill be applied)

According to a recent US study, when it comes to getting ahead in your career, it seems rude, demanding and aggressive is the way to go!

The study examined 10,000 workers across a wide range of professions, salaries and ages in the US and concluded that it really does not pay to be pleasant in the workplace. The research shows that agreeable workers earn significantly lower incomes than their more pushy colleagues. And the gap is especially wide for men. Disappointingly, the research also showed that the more agreeable you are in the workplace, the more likely you are to miss out on promotions and get loaded down with extra work.

In a 'scenario based assessment' used in the research, over 450 business students were asked to role-play as a HR manager recruiting a new employee. Following the role play, when asked why they would not hire "nice guys", the would-be human resource managers said they judged them to be "yes men" who wouldn't assert themselves in the workplace.

Psychologists however consider the research findings too simplistic. They give examples of employees who find themselves faced with impossible workloads or unreasonable demands. The agreeable employee will try to soldier on, put in as many hours as possible by themselves and just get the job done however they can. A more assertive and confident employee will ring up their boss and tell them that they are going to need more resources, more staff or more time to do the job properly. The "yes man" might think he is being a good, hard worker, but the attractiveness of sycophants for bosses wears off quickly. They will place more value and trust in the person who has the confidence and the assertiveness to tell them exactly what they need to do the job.

Psychologists also suggest that when it comes to pay or promotion, putting people in management positions where they have to make the tough, unpopular decisions or sometimes tell the boss that he or she is wrong, it is more likely that they will pick the assertive employee.

It is also important to recognise the cultural significance of this work; the research was carried out in the US, which is commonly considered to be amongst the most aggressive business cultures in the world. How do you think the results would differ in Europe or Asia?

>>

Step 4

Reflect (what have I learned?)

STOP!

By now you are likely to have gained a considerable amount of information about self-management skills and your skills related to assertiveness, prioritising and physical presentation. Your reflections may also be drawn from your experiences during your studies, other work experience you may have gained and by working through this chapter. Let's take some time to make sense of it all.

Task 1

Pick a sel-management skill (see the list at the beginning of the chapter) and write a paragraph (or two!) reflecting on your skill level.

Focus on the three key elements in your writing:

What are the key elements of the skill?

How do you typically perform related to this skill (well, average, poorly)?

>>

What training/experience have you had in this skill?

Task 2

Is the skill you've written about above representative of your skill level across the majority of self-management skills? Which skills require most development?

Task 3

Re-read your answers to Tasks 1 and 2 above. Does anything you've written surprise you?

Now you've nearly reached the end of this chapter, what do you think you've learnt about yourself and self management skills? If you are finding this difficult, imagine that you are commenting on someone else's answers to the Task 1 and 2 questions. What would you advise them about this area?

Step 5

Evaluate (reach a judgement on personal performance)

So the time has come. How do you judge/rate/score yourself at self-management? Use the information from this chapter and the previous steps to inform your decision.

Score yourself using a scale of 0 – 10 where 0 = No Skills and 10 = Highly Skilled.

Score:

Return to the Self-Assessment you undertook at the end of Chapter 1 and note the score you gave yourself then for self-management.

Self-Assessment Score:

Step 6

Check List (what next...future development)

Skill: Self-Management Skills

Area for Improvement	I need to.....	Sources of Support	Deadline
e.g. Physical presentation	..make sure I have an outfit which is suitable for the recruitment process.	Borrow items from my housemate who works in the same industry.	Insert Date

Self-Marketing Tips

Networking

The ability to network effectively is an often overlooked leadership skill, but it's one that will greatly assist you in securing the career you want.

It has been suggested that networking is simultaneously one of the most self-evident and one of the most dreaded developmental challenges that aspiring leaders must address.

Tips for Networking Effectively

Networking effectively requires getting out there and connecting with others, no matter how uncomfortable it feels. Here are some key ways you can improve your networking skills.

Hand out Business Cards

While this hardly seems like a secret, it is. The easiest step to improve your networking skills is to stash your cards everywhere - in the pockets of all your jackets, in your workout bag, in your car, you name it.

As a graduate looking for work you can get some inexpensive cards printed (there are a whole number of options online for this) which include your contact details and other relevant information such as the industry/profession you are looking to join or your degree specialisation (if it's relevant).

For example,

A. A. Smith BA (Hons) Business Management
Tel: 07920 000111
E-Mail: aasmith@email.co.uk
Skype: aasmith
Web: www.aasmith.info.uk

Be prepared to hand these out to anyone…who knows where a connection will be made that results in a new job!

Make Others Feel More Comfortable

It's important to remember that almost 80% of people are uncomfortable in networking situations. Having a host mentality, which means everything from being the person who rescues the wallflower to making sure everyone at the table is included in the conversation, makes you memorable.

Just Say Yes!

When you receive an invitation to an event, instead of making excuses why you can't go, think again. You never know when something truly amazing might happen.

A Cure for Networking Nervousness

Take someone with you such as a fellow graduate, an existing connection, colleague or friend. It beats going solo and you can be each other's backup.

Follow up Fast and Be Brief

Reliability builds your good reputation. Return phone calls or emails the following day. If you promise to do something, do it right away. Everyone is busy so send short emails. If you are sending an article or information that is more than a couple of paragraphs, highlight the key information so the recipient can scan it quickly.

Be a Connector

The true sign of a great networker is being a connector. At social and business events make a habit of introducing people to one and other if you see that they might have mutual interests or could help each other. But connecting doesn't stop when the networking event ends; do it as a matter of habit.

Self-Marketing Tips

The bonus of becoming more engaged and building a network is personal happiness and well-being. Research shows that people who are more connected are healthier and have a greater sense of well-being and happiness. So, don't do it just for career advancement; do it for your life!

“-our tip – to be more proactive! We find that some grads still think their perfect job will fall in their lap once they graduate.”

Matchtech Grads (via Twitter) www.matchtech.com

CHAPTER 10
Skills for Learning

Step 1

Review

Given the fact you may have spent around the last 15 years of your life engaged in some kind of 'formal learning' you are probably wondering why we are devoting a chapter of this guide to 'Skills for Learning'. There are three key answers to that question.

1. Given the increasing pace of change and growing complexity in the workplace, everyone is required to engage in some form of learning to at least remain effective in their job, let alone demonstrate some form of additional value which may result in rewards such as a pay rise or promotion
2. Unless you have studied 'learning' as part of your education it is unlikely that you are familiar with any of the theories of learning and have therefore never considered the related skills
3. Even if you have an understanding of learning theory and the related skills, it is important that you understand how learning in the workplace can demand new skills and a different perspective on yourself as a learner.

So given the above, it is crucial that you review your skills for learning in order to begin to plan your strategy for lifelong learning, in which your employer may play a significant role.

> *"Do some kind of work experience to formulize what kind of job you want to do, gain skills and experiences to put you strides ahead of the competition and it could lead to a permanent job."*
>
> **Prospects (via Twitter) www.prospects.ac.uk**

What is Workplace Learning?

As previously mentioned, learning in the workplace is seen as a crucial contributor to dealing with change, coping with uncertainty and complexity in the environment and creating new ideas and identifying new opportunities.

>>

Workplace learning places the whole organisation into the role of a 'unit of learning', which pushes managers into taking a strategic view of learning and thus individual employees into considering their learning needs and the impact of their learning on the business.

The **learning organisation** became of real interest in the 1990s as leaders and managers increasingly adopted the view that learning was a source of competitive advantage for their business.

Adult Learning Theory is also core to this area. Andragogy (adult learning) is a theory that holds a set of assumptions about how adults learn. Andragogy emphasises the value of the process of learning. It uses approaches to learning that are problem-based and collaborative rather than didactic, and also emphasises more equality between the 'teacher' and 'learner'.

One of the key Adult Learning theorists, Malcolm Knowles, identified the six principles of adult learning outlined below.

- Adults are internally motivated and self-directed.
- Adults bring life experiences and knowledge to learning experiences.
- Adults are goal oriented.
- Adults are relevancy oriented.
- Adults are practical.
- Adult learners like to be respected.

These principles also have considerable influence on the ways in which learning occurs in the workplace.

1. Understanding Learning

Before we spend any more time on theories related to the learning organisation and adult learning theory, it is important to acknowledge that there are two key traditions of learning that are most commonly associated with workplace learning.

>>

A. Associative Learning or Behaviourism

a) Learning in terms of responses to stimuli: automatic learning.

b) Classical conditioning.

c) Operant or instrumental conditioning.

B. Cognitive Learning

a) Insightful learning.

b) Thinking, discovering, understanding, seeing relationships and meaning.

c) New arrangements of previously learned concepts and principles.

The detail of all of this is unnecessary in a guide of this sort but it is important that you recognise that the way 'learning' is understood in the workplace shapes the way that 'learning interventions' such as training are designed and implemented.

For example, Kolb's learning cycle (on which the structure of this guide is built) is based on the premise that learning occurs through grasping an experience and transforming it into new actions based upon reflection and the emergence of new ideas. Kolb argues that the learning only happens when the cycle is complete.

Kolb's model has been highly influential in workplace learning design. Interventions are designed on the basis of individual or group learning preferences, which may allow learners to overcome their blocks to learning (this of course requires learners to be aware of those blocks!).

Kolb's model is not without its critics though and in recent years there has been a growing interest in how people learn on an everyday basis, mostly with others on an informal basis, through their participation in practice.

'Knowledge Management' is also another area of growing interest. Technology is creating an e-learning revolution, leading to new alliances between providers, new methods of delivery and the formation of communities of learners. Businesses are themselves exploring the opportunities this creates, particularly multi-site organisations who need to share learning or ensure consistency. This also requires the learners

>>

to have a degree of technology 'competence' which enables them to engage with the learning opportunities presented in this way and also feel 'comfortable' with this style of learning.

2. Aspects Of Work Based Learning

To analyse and truly understand the work based learning that takes place within any business, we typically consider three variables.

1. Learning Structure
2. Learning Strategies
3. Learning Processes (Experiences)

Learning Structure

As the structure of the organisation in which the learning takes place can have such an influence upon the design, implementation and success of the chosen intervention, we must consider the:

- size of the workplace
- number of participants (learners)
- learning experiences of the participants
- availability of learning support structures and processes
- strategic directions of the workplace
- the nature of the challenges and opportunities facing the workplace
- complexities of workplace organisation
- culture of the workplace.

Research suggests that learning structures that are customised to suit organisational cultures and are organised to match the learning requirements of individual learners result in better outcomes.

Therefore, when considering your own learning needs before accepting a new position, take a look at the learning structure of the organisation: this may be something you need to ask about at interview.

>>

Learning Strategies

Learning strategies are the specific approaches adopted by organisations to facilitate and support work-based learning. There is an array of learning strategies available which are appropriate to the needs of adult learners and suited to the organisational requirements of the workplaces in which the learning occurs.

Examples of these are:

- action learning
- mentoring
- communication networks
- facilitation
- workshops
- conferences
- networking
- off the job training
- on the job training (e.g. work shadowing).

All the learning strategies above are underpinned by adult learning principles including the following.

- Learning is an active, empowering pursuit that involves people working separately or in groups to debate issues, solve problems, develop and test solutions, and evaluate, review and refine solutions,
- Learning occurs in environments that provide relevant and meaningful contexts for personal and professional growth.
- Learning is a continuous process.

When considering any new role, take some time to understand what you will be required to learn to become effective in the role and find out about the types of learning strategy the organisation usually employs: do these strategies suit your style of learning?

>>

Learning Processes

Learning processes can be defined as the activities and experiences of individuals and groups of work-based learners. These activities and experiences are the processes through which learning is assimilated, interpreted and applied in the workplace. They result from and are supported by the collection of strategies adopted to facilitate and support learning but they impact at the personal level by allowing individuals to discuss, debate and reflect on issues and concerns.

Examples of these are:

- knowledge building
- reflection
- practice
- testing
- discussion
- debate
- team building
- critical thinking
- problem solving
- sharing.

When you consider this list, how many of these types of learning processes are you familiar with from your degree studies? How might the experience differ in the workplace? We will consider this in Step 3.

Step 2

Assess

There are many different ways to analyse yourself as a learner, some of which are far too long to be included in this guide but if you can access them provide fascinating insights!

Below is a short audit to determine whether you have a tendency towards being a visual, auditory or tactile/kinaesthetic learner.

For each item circle your response according to this key:

0 = Never

1 = Rarely

2 = Sometimes

3 = Often

4 = Always

Learning Audit						
1.	I remember something better if I write it down.	0	1	2	3	4
2.	I take detailed notes during lectures.	0	1	2	3	4
3.	When I listen, I visualise pictures, numbers, or words in my head.	0	1	2	3	4
4.	I prefer to learn with TV or video rather than other media.	0	1	2	3	4
5.	I use colour-coding to help me as I learn or work.	0	1	2	3	4
6.	I need written directions for tasks.	0	1	2	3	4
7.	I have to look at people to understand what they say.	0	1	2	3	4
8.	I understand lectures better when professors write on the board.	0	1	2	3	4

>>

9.	Charts, diagrams, and maps help me understand what someone says.	0	1	2	3	4
10.	I remember people's faces but not their names.	0	1	2	3	4
	Total (A)					
11.	I remember things better if I discuss them with someone.	0	1	2	3	4
12.	I prefer to learn by listening to a lecture rather than reading.	0	1	2	3	4
13.	I need oral directions for a task.	0	1	2	3	4
14.	Background sound helps me think.	0	1	2	3	4
15.	I like to listen to music when I study or work.	0	1	2	3	4
16.	I can understand what people say even when I cannot see them.	0	1	2	3	4
17.	I remember people's names but not their faces.	0	1	2	3	4
18.	I easily remember jokes that I hear.	0	1	2	3	4
19.	I can identify people by their voices (e.g. on the phone).	0	1	2	3	4
20.	When I turn on the TV, I listen to the sound more than I watch the screen.	0	1	2	3	4
	Total (B)					
21.	I prefer to start doing things rather than checking the directions first.	0	1	2	3	4
22.	I need frequent breaks when I work or study.	0	1	2	3	4

<<

23.	I need to eat something when I read or study.	0	1	2	3	4
24.	If I have a choice between sitting and standing, I'd rather stand.	0	1	2	3	4
25.	I get nervous when I sit still too long.					
26.	I think better when I move around (e.g. pacing or tapping my feet).	0	1	2	3	4
27.	I play with or bite on my pens during lectures.	0	1	2	3	4
28.	Manipulating objects helps me to remember what someone says.	0	1	2	3	4
29.	I move my hands when I speak.	0	1	2	3	4
30.	I draw lots of pictures (doodles) in my notebook during lectures.	0	1	2	3	4
	Total (C)					

Once you have totalled your points, write the results in the blanks below. Circle the higher number in each part (if they are close, circle both). Read about your learning styles on the next page.

A = Visual

B = Auditory

C = Tactile/Kinaesthetic

If you came out as more visual than auditory, you rely more on the sense of sight, and you learn best through visual means (books, video, charts, pictures). If you are more auditory, you prefer listening and speaking activities (discussions, lectures, audiotapes, role-plays). If you have a tactile/kinaesthetic style preference, you benefit from doing projects, working with objects, and moving around (playing games, building models, conducting experiments).

>>

Step 3

Application (how might skill be applied)

It has been reported recently that Boots UK is launching a new 18-month business apprenticeship programme for students who have completed their A-levels.

During the programme, successful applicants will carry out placements in various business functions throughout the Nottingham support office, as well as in-store, to further expand their skills and experience.

Candidates will have the opportunity to take on a job with real responsibilities within the UK's leading pharmacy led health and beauty retailer, providing invaluable experience into the workplace whilst learning how the retail industry works. Boots will also fund and fully support candidates to study for a Higher Apprenticeship in Business Management, equivalent to a foundation degree level.

Sarah White, head of capability at Boots UK's Nottingham support office said: "At Boots we're passionate about attracting and developing the best new talent. This apprenticeship programme is for young people who are beginning to evaluate their career options after their A-levels and would prefer to enter the workplace."

Alex Gourlay, chief executive of the health and beauty division, Alliance Boots, said: "We are committed to supporting the employment and further education of young people. Our Boots Business Apprenticeship Programme complements our existing work with Business in the Community, Work Inspiration Week, Young Enterprise and our range of employment, education and training for young people and existing colleagues."

The article also suggests that Boots UK utilises a range of other workplace learning strategies, alongside the apprenticeships, to develop their workforce. These include on-the-job support, training and mentoring.

The design of this programme of learning, including formal off-the-job training (Higher Apprenticeship in Business Management) along with formal on-the-job training will also be supplemented by a range of informal, often unrecognised, learning strategies such as the information shared between peer apprentices as they make their way through the formal programme. The value of such a variety of learning strategies is

>>

<<

not to be underestimated and the demands it makes on the learner are also to be acknowledged: the investment by both the organisation and the learner is significant but the potential rewards equally valuable.

Unfortunately, many organisations do not have the resources or expertise to invest in this way in their new employees and therefore more onus is placed upon the new employee to seek out ways of learning that will benefit them professionally and their employer. However, given the earlier points made about the value of employees who are open to learning it would have to be a somewhat unenlightened employer who wouldn't seek to support your relevant learning aspirations in some way.

In fact, the right to request time to train applies across the UK to employees in all organisations with at least 250 employees. Employees' requests can be to undertake accredited programmes leading to a qualification, or for unaccredited training to help them develop specific skills relevant to their job, workplace or business. While employee requests may involve agreeing time away from their duties, the primary focus of the new right is about agreeing relevant training for staff.

Step 4

Reflect (what have I learned?)

STOP!

By now you are likely to have gained a considerable amount of information about the skills for learning and yourself as a learner from your experiences during your studies, other work experience you may have gained and by working through this chapter. Let's take some time to make sense of it all.

<<

Task 1

Pick an example of formal learning in which you've been involved and write a paragraph (or two!) describing the experience below.

Focus on the three key elements in your writing:

Learning Structure
Learning Strategy
Learning Process

>>

<<

Task 2

Looking back on this example, what skills did you need to employ to ensure your learning was successful?

Task 3

What kind of workplace learner do you think you will be? What will the greatest challenges be?

Step 5

Evaluate (reach a judgement on personal performance)

So the time has come. How do you judge/rate/score yourself as a learner? Use the information from this chapter and the previous steps to inform your decision.

Score yourself using a scale of 0 – 10 where 0 = No Skills and 10 = Highly Skilled.

Score:

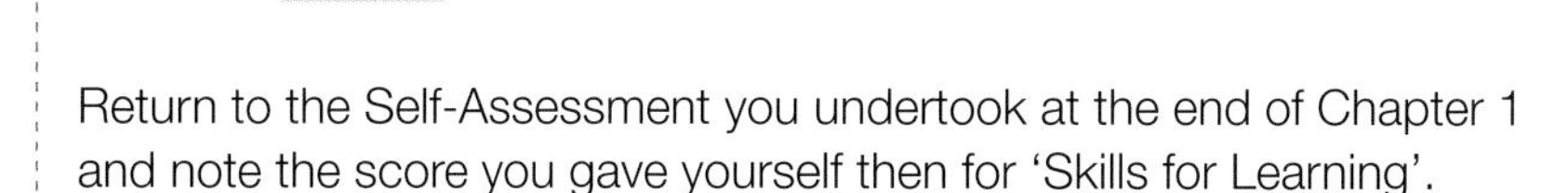

Return to the Self-Assessment you undertook at the end of Chapter 1 and note the score you gave yourself then for 'Skills for Learning'.

Self-Assessment Score:

Step 6

Check List (what next...future development)

Skill: Skills for Learning

Area for Improvement	**I need to.....**	**Sources of Support**	**Deadline**
e.g. Identify my learning blocks	..reflect further on myself as a learner to identify the blocks.	Speak to my former tutor to gain their input.	Insert Date

Self-Marketing Tips

Online

Your online identity is constructed by any online content (on the internet) that relates to you as an individual. 'Managing' your online identity can be critical when looking for work. Think of your online presence as your personal brand. It is therefore important that you consider how you promote yourself or opportunities may pass you by. Equally, you can use that personal brand you create in the online environment to attract interest from potential employers!

An online identity is portrayed through social networking profiles, business networking files, blogging or tweeting, news items and any other online content that is attributed or related to you.

Personal Branding Online – Top Tips!

Review all of the ways in which you engage with the online environment. List them here:

Are some of these ways purely personal (for fun, to engage with friends etc)? If so, then the information you share here should not be publicly available and therefore not available to potential employers. Check that your privacy settings reflect this.

Self-Marketing Tips

IF YOU CANNOT GUARANTEE THAT THE INFORMATION IS NOT PUBLICALLY AVAILABLE THEN YOU NEED TO SERIOUSLY CONSIDER ITS IMPACT ON YOUR PERSONAL BRAND!

- It's a good idea to appear fun-loving and socially active on networking sights such as Facebook. However, try and avoid any content where you are having a little too much fun. Things like breaking the law, excessive drinking/drugs and nudity will turn employers off. Do not let yourself become associated with this sort of thing.
- Try to avoid any controversial content. This can range from a silly political joke that seemed funny at the time to a heated anonymous blog. It's not about changing your personality or views, its just that websites may not be the best way to publish them. Try also to avoid overly sexual content and swearing.
- Use your profile on social networking sites as an online CV. Promote yourself through the activities that you do which align with the skills and competences that potential employers may be looking for! Also many networking sites allow you to list previous employers which is an indication of your experience.

LinkedIn

If you have not already, sign up for a LinkedIn account (www.linkedin.com). LinkedIn is an online networking site for professionals. Even if you do not have any contacts to start with you will quickly find more as you proceed through the graduate recruitment process and into your first job.

CHAPTER 11

Emotional Intelligence

Step 1

Review

What is Emotional Intelligence?

Early theories of Emotional Intelligence (often known as 'EQ' or 'EI') were first published in the 1990s, partly as a response to the dominance of 'IQ' as a measure of intelligence. All emotional intelligence abilities involve some degree of skill in the affective domain, along with skill in whatever cognitive elements are also at play in each ability. Early EI theories sought to explore the limitations of measuring intelligence as a purely cognitive process and instead recognise the relationship between thought and feeling and therefore the impact of emotion on performance.

Following the early theorists' work, it was US psychologist Daniel Goleman in the mid to late 90s who really began to explore the impact of EI in the organizational (work-related) domain.

According to Goleman, all the EI models share a common core of basic concepts. Emotional intelligence, at the most general level, refers to **the abilities to recognise and regulate emotions in ourselves and in others**. This definition suggests four major EI domains.

- Self-Awareness
- Self-Management
- Social Awareness
- Relationship Management

Given the importance attached to 'Self-Management' skills by employers, this domain warrants a chapter of its own in this guide. Therefore, this chapter focuses on the remaining three domains to ensure you understand their importance in developing and demonstrating your emotional intelligence.

>>

1. Self Awareness

Self-awareness is commonly understood to be the ability to recognise and understand your moods, emotions, and drives, as well as their effect on others.

The following are key indicators of self-awareness.

- Self-confidence
- Realistic self-assessment
- Self-deprecating sense of humour

Self-awareness is the basis for the other components of emotional intelligence. It refers to a person's capacity for being aware of how they are feeling. In general, more self-awareness allows us to more effectively guide our own lives and behaviour.

Being aware of emotions requires reflection. This in itself is a skill that this guide has certainly enabled you to work on – in each chapter Step 4 has challenged you to reflect on what you've learned and then consider how this might help you in the future.

The recommendation from psychologists is that if one learns to pause, to focus inward, and to seek one's emotions, one can become more aware of them. You might begin asking yourself several times during a normal day, "What am I feeling now?" If you question yourself frequently for a week, you will probably be able to notice what you feel more readily. Then the challenge – one accepted by people with high emotional intelligence – is to manage those emotions in a more positive way. It has been found that people who develop a high emotional intelligence do not yield to their emotions easily; rather they seek to manage them.

In summary, emotional awareness is:

A. Recognising one's emotions and their effects. People with this competence:

   - know which emotions they are feeling and why
   - recognise how their feelings affect their performance
   - have a guiding awareness of their values and goals.

<<

B. Conducting accurate self-assessment, which is knowing one's strengths and limits. People with this competence are:

- aware of their strengths and weaknesses
- reflective, learning from experience
- open to candid feedback, new perspectives, continuous learning, and self-development
- able to show a sense of humour and perspective about themselves.

C. Being self-confident by possessing a 'sureness' about one's self-worth and capabilities. People with this competence:

- present themselves with self-assurance; have "presence"
- can voice views that are unpopular and go out on a limb for what is right
- are decisive, able to make sound decisions despite uncertainties and pressures.

" *1. Have self awareness. 2. Do your research. 3. Show your potential with facts 4. Enjoy the experience - all add up one day!* "

Unilever Grads UK (via Twitter)
http://www.unilever.co.uk/careers/whyunilever/graduates/index.aspx

2. Social Awareness

Social awareness is the ability to sense, understand, and react to others' emotions while comprehending social networks.

This seems of particular relevance in the workplace when we explore this in more detail.

- Understanding Others: Sensing others' feelings and perspectives and taking an active interest in their concerns.

>>

- Developing others: Sensing others' development needs and encouraging their abilities.
- Service orientation: Anticipating, recognising and meeting customers' needs.
- Leveraging diversity: Cultivating opportunities through different kinds of people.
- Political awareness: Reading a group's emotional currents and power relationships.

Recent research by Time magazine in the US, has found that undergraduates have less empathy - the ability to understand and share the feelings of others - than students of previous generations.

Digital communication, social networking, video conferencing and other forms of new media are being blamed for this loss of empathy.

After all, it's much easier to say negative things about others if you don't have to say it to their face. And if I don't feel like engaging in your problems, I can simply log off, or even 'unfriend' you. It's an easy option.

The trouble is that when there is no empathy, when we don't work to understand the needs of others, there is also a significant loss of trust.

"Because I don't really know what you're thinking and feeling I trust you less, and isolate myself more." This can have major implications for business where trust is essential for successful leadership and partnerships.

More importantly though, when you respond to the needs and feelings of other people, you gain their trust. Others will be labelled uncaring and insensitive, but you are trusted when you're able to understand and respond to the needs and values of individuals, and the group. This is true whether you're a salesperson dealing with the public, or a leader in an organisation.

Leaders in organisations have traditionally viewed empathy with suspicion, thinking that there is no place for soft emotional skills in the tough world of business. However, in recent years there is a growing understanding of the importance of emotional intelligence. Changing times and recognition of the strategic advantages of taking employees' feelings into consideration has led to social consciousness being regarded as a critical skill for effective leaders.

>>

<<

This has even impacted the training given to doctors. Today doctors are trained to formulate a bio-psycho-social understanding of the problem rather than treating patients purely as a diagnosis.

Empathising with someone - understanding their point of view - doesn't mean you have to agree with their point of view. Empathy is really about acknowledging the emotions of others, being thoughtful and considerate of their feelings, and making decisions that take those feelings into consideration.

3. Relationship Management

'Relationships' are considered to be one of the key areas in which businesses are seeking to develop in the 21st century; relationships between leaders and their teams, between peers, across the supply chain, in strategic alliances and partnerships and with customers and clients amongst many other forms of relationships. Relationships are typically considered to be one of the cornerstones of sustainable business. It is no longer enough to think of business as a series of transactions in this increasingly competitive global marketplace

According to EI theories, relationships are based on the following:

- caring behaviour
- showing interest
- fairness
- demonstrating trustworthiness
- demonstrating understanding
- behaving as a change catalyst
- effective conflict management
- teamwork and
- cooperation.

As you will note, we have chapters in this guide on conflict management and teamworking also. Such is the importance of emotional intelligence in enhancing your employability.

>>

Step 2

Assess

Use the following diagnostic tool to assess your emotional intelligence. This tool is based on Goleman's Emotional Competence Inventory 2.0.

Put a score (0-10) in the box next to each of the descriptors that relate to the four domains of emotional intelligence. You are scoring your own skills and behaviour in each of these areas.

REMEMBER - The more honest your assessment here the more value you will gain from this whole process.

Factor	Score (0-10)
SELF-AWARENESS	
Emotional Awareness: Recognising one's emotions and their effects	
Accurate Self-Assessment: Knowing one's strengths and limits	
Self-Confidence: A strong sense of one's self-worth and capabilities	
Self-Awareness Total:	
SELF-MANAGEMENT	n/a
Emotional Self-Control: Keeping disruptive emotions and impulses in check	
Transparency: Maintaining integrity, acting congruently with one's values	
Adaptability: Flexibility in handling change	
Achievement: Striving to improve or meeting a standard of excellence	

>>

Initiative: Readiness to act on opportunities	
Optimism: Persistence in pursuing goals despite obstacles and setbacks	
Self-Management Total:	
SOCIAL AWARENESS	
Empathy: Sensing others' feelings and perspectives, and taking an active interest in their concerns	
Organizational Awareness: Reading a group's emotional currents and power relationships	
Service Orientation: Anticipating, recognizing, and meeting customers' needs	
Social Awareness Total:	
RELATIONSHIP MANAGEMENT	
Developing Others: Sensing others' development needs and bolstering their abilities	
Inspirational Leadership: Inspiring and guiding individuals and groups	
Change Catalyst: Initiating or managing change	
Influence: Wielding effective tactics for persuasion	
Conflict Management: Negotiating and resolving disagreements	
Teamwork & Collaboration: Working with others toward shared goals. Creating group synergy in pursuing collective goals.	
Relationship Management Total:	
EMOTIONAL INTELLIGENCE TOTAL (OUT OF 40):	

<<

Let's take a moment to look at the results.

Transcribe your scores below for each domain:

Self-Awareness score:

Self-Management score:

Social Awareness score:

Relationship Management score:

When we come to reflect in Step 4 it will be useful to understand in which domain you are strongest and which domain needs work!

Were there also any exceptions within any of the domains; any descriptors where you scored particularly high or particularly low?

We'll come back to this later!

Step 3

Application (how might skill be applied)

According to a reporter writing recently on the lack of British women in the Forbes 100 Most Powerful Women 2011 list, there have been calls from many quarters for a greater female presence at the highest levels of business. According to the article women are thought to bring diplomacy and understanding to the workplace because of their emotional intelligence. The Dalai Lama, on his visit to US President Barack Obama last year, joined the chorus for more women to be offered top management roles because they are "more sensitive to suffering".

A recent study of emotional intelligence was conducted on three hundred and fifty-eight Managers across the Johnson & Johnson

>>

Consumer & Personal Care Group (JJC&PC Group) globally to assess if there were specific leadership competencies that distinguished high performers from average performers.

Participants were randomly selected, then coded for performance rating, potential code, gender, functional group and regional area. More than fourteen hundred employees took part in a one hundred and eighty three question multi-rater survey that measured a variety of competencies associated with leadership performance including those commonly referred to as Emotional Intelligence.

Results showed that the highest performing managers have significantly more "emotional competence" than other managers. There was strong inter-rater agreement among Supervisors, Peers, and Subordinates that the competencies of Self-Confidence, Achievement Orientation, Initiative, Leadership, Influence and Change Catalyst differentiate superior performers. The high potential managers received higher scores in the emotional competencies by Peers and Supervisors, but not by Subordinates. Some gender difference was found, with Supervisors rating Females higher in Adaptability and Service Orientation, while Peers rated Females higher on Emotional Self-Awareness, Conscientiousness, Developing Others, Service Orientation, and Communication. Direct reports scored Males higher in Change Catalyst.

Given the results of this and many other similar research projects in the workplace, it is clear that awareness of the role of emotional intelligence on performance is growing. Recruiters may increasingly look for ways to assess emotional intelligence and therefore by providing evidence of it in your application you are demonstrating your awareness of its value to them as your potential employer and your commitment to continually developing your emotional intelligence throughout your career.

Step 4

Reflect (what have I learned?)

STOP!

By now you are likely to have gained a considerable amount of information about emotional intelligence. Let's take some time to make sense of it all.

Task 1

Returning to the diagnostic tool in Step 2, take a moment to transcribe your results for each domain below:

Self-Awareness score:

Self-Management score:

Social Awareness score:

Relationship Management score:

In which domain did you score highest? Why do you think this is the case?

In which domain did you score the lowest? Why do you think this is the case?

Were there any descriptors that scored particularly high or low? Note the descriptor(s) here

Why do you think you scored them in this way?

Task 2

Looking back on Task 1 and other feedback you've had on the domains covered within emotional intelligence, how do you feel about your level of emotional intelligence?

Task 3

Your own perception of your level of emotional intelligence may well be very different from others' perception. Create a blank copy of the tool in Step 2 and ask a trusted peer or manager to score you against each of the descriptors.

Note their scores for you below:

Self-Awareness score:

Self-Management score:

Social Awareness score:

Relationship Management score:

<<

How do these scores compare to your own scores? Why might this be the case?

Step 5

Evaluate (reach a judgement on personal performance)

So the time has come. How do you judge/rate/score your emotional intelligence skills? Use the information from this chapter and the previous steps to inform your decision.

Score yourself using a scale of 0 – 10 where 0 = No Skills and 10 = Highly Skilled.

Score:

Return to the Self-Assessment you undertook at the end of Chapter 1 and note the score you gave yourself then for emotional intelligence.

Self-Assessment Score:

>>

<<

Do these scores differ? If so, why do you think this might be?

Step 6

Check List (what next...future development)

Skill: Emotional Intelligence			
Area for Improvement	**I need to.....**	**Sources of Support**	**Deadline**
e.g. Caring	..find ways to demonstrate I care about my colleagues.	Observe how my 'caring' colleagues do this.	Insert Date

As always, if applying for an 'advertised' position it is important to thoroughly analyse the advertisement before you begin; to identify the skills that are explicitly required (some may be considered Essential and some Desirable but nevertheless they want them all!!).

So what reference to emotional intelligence (or its domains) do they make in the advertisement?

In carrying out your further research about the organisation, what mention do they make of emotional intelligence?

CV/Resume

Depending on the approach you've taken with your CV/Resume there are a number of ways in which you can highlight your emotional intelligence.

- Give examples from each of the four domains of emotional intelligence when writing up any part-time work or evidence from study experiences.
- Use language that illustrates your emotional intelligence in your personal profile at the start of your CV/resume.
- If you choose to include hobbies or interests on your CV/resume, highlight those which demonstrate emotional intelligence such as team sports or community activities.

CHAPTER 12

Entrepreneurship and Consultancy

Step 1

Review

1. Entrepreneurship

A recent report from the World Economic Forum suggests that just 1% of start up businesses account for 40% of new jobs created. Business start-ups are at the very core of the economic growth agenda and therefore developing the skills required for entrepreneurship is highly desirable.

However, this is not the only argument for developing entrepreneurial skills. Organisations in both the private and public sectors are increasingly recognising the value of entrepreneurial skills amongst their workforce.

> "Better to have played & lost than never to have played at all. Forget perfection & get as many of your applications out as possible"
>
> The Graduate Game (via Twitter). www.graduategame.com

The entrepreneurial process itself is comprised of three parts over which the entrepreneur exerts control/influence:

- the opportunity
- the organisation
- the resources.

It is the entrepreneur's responsibility to:

- ensure the organisation is able to maximise the opportunity
- ensure the resources within the organisation are configured to maximise the opportunity
- ensure the resources available are focused on maximising the opportunity.

>>

So what skills are required to achieve this? Some of the key ones are:

- analytical skills: for example, to analyse the market, identify potential opportunities, interpret sales figures etc
- negotiation skills: for example, to reduce costs, agree improved terms and conditions
- numeracy skills: for example, to be able to 'read' the financial reports of the business
- communication skills: for example, to communicate effectively with customers, staff and other stakeholders
- networking skills: for example, to build relationships with potential suppliers, to partner with companies who target your same market segment
- creative skills: for example, to come up with your business idea in the first place, to deal with problems that occur whilst running your business.

2. Consultancy

Companies and organisations hire consultants to strategise solutions to business, organisational, or industry specific problems. The value in hiring a consultant is a fresh perspective, objectivity, and/or a specific knowledge base or expertise.

The Consulting Industry can be divided into the following areas.

Management Consulting: Focus is on how a company or organisation works to achieve its stated goals. This can include working on strategy, operations, and information technology.

Strategy Consulting: Focus is on identifying the direction, goals, and growth of a company or organisation within a specific industry.

Information Technology (IT) Consulting: Focus is on using technology to help an organisation become more efficient and achieve its goals.

Industry Specific Consulting: Focus is on a specific industry and can include strategy, management, IT, scientific or technical consulting.

<<

Skills typically required in consultancy include:

- problem solving
- researching
- analytical and quantitative thinking
- understanding of business
- interpersonal and communication skills
- networking
- ability to work in a fast-paced environment
- project management.

Step 2

Assess

Undertake some research of real life 'business start-ups' and create a list below of the skills that the entrepreneurs need to possess or develop to be successful.

You can find case studies and articles in all broadsheet newspapers and standard business journals to help you with this.

Entrepreneur 1:	
Skill	
Skill	
Skill	

Entrepreneur 2:	
Skill	
Skill	
Skill	

>>

<<

Entrepreneur 3:	
Skill	
Skill	
Skill	

Put a tick (✔) in one or both columns (ignore the 'Me' column for now).

Skills Required	Start-Up	Expansion	Me
Problem solving			
Analysing facts and situations			
Applying creative thinking to develop appropriate solutions			
Decision making			
Handle data			
Draw conclusions			
Manipulation of numbers			
General mathematical awareness			
Application in practical contexts (e.g. measuring, weighing)			
Innovative approach			
Creative thinking			
Fresh knowledge			
Challenging assumptions			
Relationship building/ Networking			
Respecting others			

>>

<<

Skills Required	Start-Up	Expansion	Me
Cooperating			
Negotiating/persuading/ influencing			
Contributing to discussions			
Awareness of interdependence with others			
Motivating others			
Leadership			

Now consider your own skills against those required and put a tick (✔) in the 'Me' column if you believe you already possess that particular skill.

REMEMBER - The more honest your assessment here the more value you will gain from this whole process.

Of the skills that you consider to be required (in the table above) are there any that you do not possess or require some development?

Note them below.

Step 3

Application (how might skill be applied)

According to a new report from the Government of the Future Centre the European economy could be grown by €1.2 trillion ($A1.6 trillion) and 15 million new jobs could be created if public sector entrepreneurship was encouraged.

Both in the private and public sector the development of entrepreneurial skills are increasingly encouraged:

- to generate new products and services

- to find solutions for problems and challenges
- to identify ways for generating greater value for customers
- to promote efficiency in the provision of public services, and
- to seek out cost savings (both in terms of company budgets and the public purse).

More and more companies are also sourcing external consultants or developing internal consultancy competencies across the span of their businesses.

The Management Consultancies Association reported that in 2010 the UK consulting industry returned to growth, despite the significant drop in public sector consultancy work. The focus of the new work in both sectors appears to be opportunity identification.

Companies are also encouraging and supporting entrepreneurship throughout their supply chain (partners, suppliers etc.) in order to reap the benefits this returns to their own organisation.

Coca-cola, one of the world's most geographically dispersed multinationals, recognizes the value of the mutual dependency that exists between themselves and the other businesses in their supply chain. In the US alone they invest over $10bn per annum in their supply chain, which has a significant impact upon the small and medium businesses who make up the supply chain. Their chairman and CEO even recognises that the support of entrepreneurship is one of Coca-cola's key responsibilities.

Step 4

Reflect (what have I learned?)

STOP!

By now you are likely to have gained a considerable amount of information about entrepreneurship and consultancy and your skills in both of these areas, from your experiences during your studies, other work experience you may have gained and by working through this chapter. Let's take some time to make sense of it all.

>>

<<

Task 1

Pick one of the specific skills required by entrepreneurs or consultants and review a time when you've had to use this skill.

Is this example 'typical' of your use of this skill? If not, what makes it different?

Task 2

Looking back on this and other experiences of using this skill you've had, how do you feel about this skill?

>>

Task 3

Re-read your answers to Tasks 1 and 2 above. Does anything you've written surprise you?

Now you've nearly reached the end of this chapter, what do you think you've learnt about entrepreneurship and consultancy and your skills in these areas? If you are finding this difficult, imagine that you are commenting on someone else's answers to the Task 1 and 2 questions.

What would you advise them about entrepreneurship and consultancy?

Step 5

Evaluate (reach a judgement on personal performance)

So the time has come. How do you judge/rate/score yourself as a potential entrepreneur or consultant? Use the information from this chapter and the previous steps to inform your decision.

Score yourself using a scale of 0 – 10 where 0 = No Skills and 10 = Highly Skilled.

Score:

Return to the Self-Assessment you undertook at the end of Chapter 1 and note the score you gave yourself then for entrepreneurship and consultancy.

Self-Assessment Score:

Step 6

Check List (what next...future development)

Skill: Entrepreneurship and Consultancy

Area for Improvement	I need to.....	Sources of Support	Deadline
e.g. Creative thinking	..be more innovative when solving problems.	Ask trusted friends/colleagues to help me debate ideas.	Insert Date

Self-Marketing Tips

"Don't wait for an employer or a paycheck before starting your career. Intern, volunteer, or find a way to create your own job in your desired field for real experience. (For instance, a blog related to your future career is a great way to start establishing a professional profile.)"

Charles Purdy, Senior Editor, MonsterCareers (via Twitter)
www.monster.com

'Creativity' is a core skill for entrepreneurs and the ability to bring a 'fresh perspective' is also critical for consultants. In marketing yourself to potential employers or clients this can also be true.

If you really want your application to stand out from the rest (and remember we are currently facing market conditions where there are high numbers of applications for almost all graduate positions) then it's time to be creative!

I am not saying let's go crazy and hire a clown to personally deliver your CV whilst singing a song about you, but find professional ways to enhance the presentation of your application or get creative about the ways in which you build relationships with potential clients or employers.

Self-Marketing Tips

For example

- What is the house style used by the company in their corporate branding? Can you employ the colours/fonts etc in your application?
- As well as sending a written covering letter explaining why you are so interested in the position, record yourself in a short video telling them why you want to work for them and attach it to your email.

So, what would work in the industry sector you are looking to join?

I heard a story recently about a successful consultant in North America who had been trying for many years to secure a contract with a particular organisation. He happened to know that the CEO of the company was a New York Yankees fan and that they had a big game coming up when he himself would next be in New York that the CEO was unable to attend. So he bought a ticket to the game, took a photo of himself in the stands and then couriered the photo along with a hot dog bought from one of the vendors at the game overnight to the CEO offering him the opportunity to meet and discuss the game he'd missed.

Self-Marketing Tips

The CEO's Personal Assistant was on the telephone immediately to arrange a meeting and the consultant has had a number of contracts with the company since.

Once again researching the company and finding out about key decision makers can be key to your success in securing a position.

> "The best way to predict the future is to create it."
>
> Peter Drucker

Useful Links – Entrepreneurship

The Institute for Small Business and Entrepreneurship – www.isbe.org.uk

www.startups.co.uk

UK Entrepreneurship Club – www.ukeclub.org

Enterprise UK – www.enterpriseuk.org

How to become an entrepreneur – www.entrepreneursuk.net

Further Reading – Entrepreneurship

Wickham, P A (2006), Strategic Entrepreneurship, 4th Edition, FT Prentice Hall, Essex [ISBN 0-273-70642-X]

Deschamps, J P (2008), Innovation Leaders, Jossey-Bass, Chichester [ISBN-10: 0470515244]

Bennis, W, Spreitzer, G and Cummings T G (Eds) (2001), The Future of Leadership, Jossey-Bass, San Francisco

Deschamps, J P (2008), Innovation Leaders, Jossey-Bass, Chichester

Maital, S and Seshadri, DVR (2007), Innovation Management, Sage, India

Northouse, P G (2007), Leadership: Theory and Practice, 4th Edition, Sage, London

Shane, S (2003), A General Theory of Entrepreneurship, Edward Elgar, Cheltenham

Smilor, R W & Sexton, D L (1996), Leadership and Entrepreneurship, Quorum, Westport CT

Swedberg, R (Ed) (2000), Entrepreneurship: The Social Science View, Oxford University Press, Oxford

Useful Links - Consultancy

Management Consultancy Association – www.mca.org.uk

Association of Internal Management Consultants – www.aimc.org

Association of Management Consulting Firms – www.amcf.org

Institute of Management Consultants USA – www.imcua.org

Consulting Central - www.consultingcentral.com

Consulting Information Services, LLC

www.consultinginfo.com/ Consulting Magazine

www.consultingmag.com/ Hoovers Online

premium.hoovers.com/ Kennedy Information

www.kennedyinfo.com/mc/mcindex.html

The Vault - http://www.vault.com/hubs/industrylist.jsp

Self-Marketing Tips

Further Reading – Consultancy

Consultancy Magazine www.consultingmag.com/

Flawless Consulting: A Guide to Getting Your Expertise Used, (Peter Block, 2000).

How to Make It Big As a Consultant, (William Cohen, 1991).

Management Consulting: A Guide to the Profession, (Milan Kubr, 2002)

Management Consulting: A Complete Guide to the Industry, (Sugata Biswas and Daryl Twitchell, 2002)

The Fast Track: The Insider's Guide to Winning Jobs in Management Consulting, Investment Banking, and Securities Trading, (Mariam Naficy, 1997)

The McKinsey Mind, (Ethan Rasiel, 2002).

The Seven Cs of Consulting: The Definitive Guide to the Consulting Process, (Mick Cope, 2003)

Vault Guide to the Top 50 Management and Strategy Consulting Firms, (Vault, 2004 6th edition)

What Management Is: How It Works and Why It's Everyone's Business, (Joan Magretta & Nan Stone, 2002).

Appendix: Employability Skills Mapping

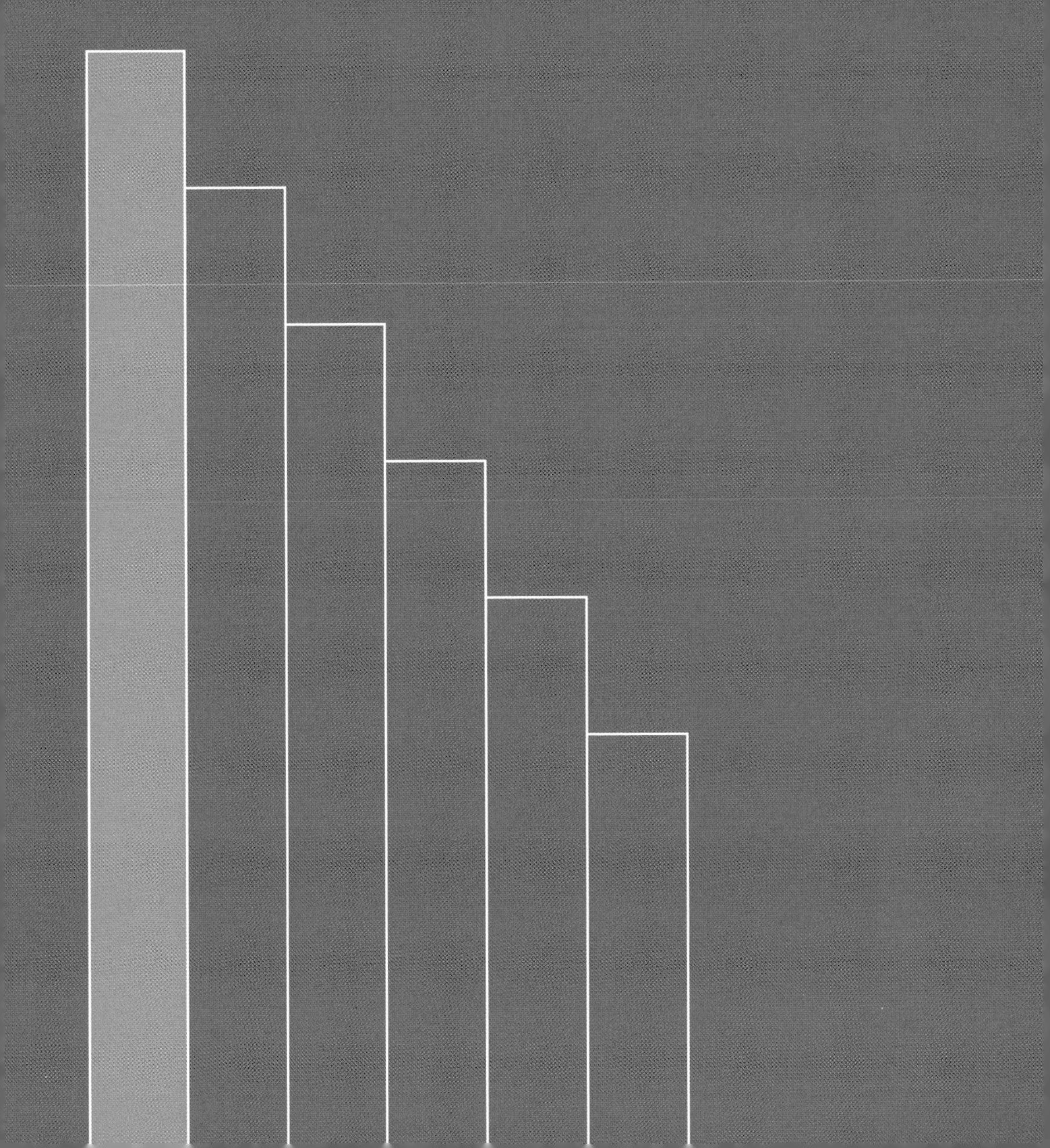

Employability Skills Mapping

SKILL	SOURCE	CBI Website 13/04/11	EC Report Graduate Employability 11/10	Dearing Report (1997)	Eurobarometer on Graduate Employability 12/10
Self-Management		✓			
Readiness to accept responsibility		✓			
Flexibility		✓			
Resilience		✓			
Appropriate assertiveness		✓			
Time management		✓			
Readiness to improve performance based on feedback/reflective learning		✓			
Planning/organisational skills			✓		
Contingency planning					
Ability to prioritise effectively					
Learning how to learn				✓	
Emotional Intelligence					
Personal appearance					
Courage					

		✓					✓								**Higher Education Academy & CIHE: Student Employability Profiles (2006)**
								✓							**Learning Skills Network: Employability Skills Explored (2008)**
✓				✓	✓	✓	✓	✓							**PWC: Being the one with the foot in the door (2010)**
															Specialist Schools and Academies Trust: Applied Learning Making Learning Work
															UKCES Ambition 2020 07/05/09
	✓			✓			✓	✓	✓	✓		✓	✓		**UKCES The Employability Challenge 02/09**
				✓		✓	✓				✓				**HECSU, ACGAS: What do Graduates do? (2010)**

Employability Skills Mapping

SKILL	SOURCE	CBI Website 13/04/11	EC Report Graduate Employability 11/10	Dearing Report (1997)	Eurobarometer on Graduate Employability 12/10
Self-Management (Cont)					
Integrity					
Manage conflict					
Working under pressure					
Work ethic					
Willingness to ask for help					
Self-awareness					
Self-reliant					
Teamworking		✓	✓		✓
Respecting others		✓			
Cooperating		✓			
Negotiating/persuading/influencing		✓			
Contributing to discussions		✓			
Awareness of interdependence with others		✓			
Motivating others					
Leadership					

Higher Education Academy & CIHE: Student Employability Profiles (2006)										✓			✓				
Learning Skills Network: Employability Skills Explored (2008)																	
PWC: Being the one with the foot in the door (2010)			✓	✓	✓					✓			✓			✓	
Specialist Schools and Academies Trust: Applied Learning Making Learning Work			✓			✓				✓							
UKCES Ambition 2020 07/05/09													✓				
UKCES The Employability Challenge 02/09							✓			✓		✓	✓		✓		
HECSU, ACGAS: What do Graduates do? (2010)								✓	✓	✓			✓			✓	✓

APPENDIX

Employability Skills Mapping

	SOURCE	CBI Website 13/04/11	EC Report Graduate Employability 11/10	Dearing Report (1997)	Eurobarometer on Graduate Employability 12/10
SKILL					
Business and customer awareness		✓			
Basic understanding of the key drivers for business success		✓			
Importance of innovation		✓			
Calculated risk taking		✓			
Need to provide customer satisfaction		✓			
Building customer loyalty		✓			
Sector specific skills			✓		
Technical skills					
Commercial/Financial awareness					
Budget management					
Awareness of stakeholder needs					
Understanding of contribution of own role to organisation					
Problem Solving		✓	✓		
Analysing facts and situations		✓	✓		
Applying creative thinking to develop appropriate solutions		✓			

	✓	✓				✓	✓				✓		✓	✓		**Higher Education Academy & CIHE: Student Employability Profiles (2006)**
																Learning Skills Network: Employability Skills Explored (2008)
					✓	✓	✓	✓		✓				✓		**PWC: Being the one with the foot in the door (2010)**
																Specialist Schools and Academies Trust: Applied Learning Making Learning Work
		✓														**UKCES Ambition 2020 07/05/09**
✓	✓	✓	✓	✓							✓	✓		✓		**UKCES The Employability Challenge 02/09**
		✓					✓	✓		✓	✓			✓		**HECSU, ACGAS: What do Graduates do? (2010)**

Employability Skills Mapping

SKILL	SOURCE	CBI Website 13/04/11	EC Report Graduate Employability 11/10	Dearing Report (1997)	Eurobarometer on Graduate Employability 12/10
Problem Solving (Cont)					
Decision making			✓		
Handle Data					
Draw Conclusions					
Communication and Literacy		✓	✓	✓	✓
Application of literacy		✓			
Ability to produce clear, structured written work		✓	✓		
Oral literacy (listening and questioning)		✓			
Foreign language skills			✓		✓
Presentation skills					
Application of Numeracy		✓	✓	✓	
Manipulation of numbers		✓			
General mathematical awareness		✓			
Application in practical contexts (e.g. measuring, weighing)		✓			

Higher Education Academy & CIHE: Student Employability Profiles (2006)				✓	✓	✓									
Learning Skills Network: Employability Skills Explored (2008)						✓						✓			
PWC: Being the one with the foot in the door (2010)							✓	✓	✓		✓				
Specialist Schools and Academies Trust: Applied Learning Making Learning Work						✓									
UKCES Ambition 2020 07/05/09						✓									
UKCES The Employability Challenge 02/09						✓			✓			✓			
HECSU, ACGAS: What do Graduates do? (2010)			✓						✓	✓	✓	✓			

Employability Skills Mapping

SOURCE		CBI Website 13/04/11	EC Report Graduate Employability 11/10	Dearing Report (1997)	Eurobarometer on Graduate Employability 12/10
SKILL					
Application of Information Technology		✓		✓	
Basic IT skills (word processing, spreadsheets, file management and use of internet search engines)		✓			
Positive Attitude		✓			
'Can do' approach		✓			
Readiness to take part and contribute		✓			
Openness to new ideas		✓			
Ability to make suggestions					
Drive to make things happen		✓			
Adaptive (new situations)			✓		✓
Enthusiasm					
Commitment					
Reliability					
Desire to finish the job					
Self starting		✓			
Resourceful					

	✓	✓												✓		Higher Education Academy & CIHE: Student Employability Profiles (2006)
				✓												Learning Skills Network: Employability Skills Explored (2008)
				✓	✓	✓	✓		✓	✓						PWC: Being the one with the foot in the door (2010)
			✓													Specialist Schools and Academies Trust: Applied Learning Making Learning Work
														✓		UKCES Ambition 2020 07/05/09
								✓	✓	✓		✓		✓		UKCES The Employability Challenge 02/09
✓	✓			✓	✓		✓							✓		HECSU, ACGAS: What do Graduates do? (2010)

Employability Skills Mapping

SKILL \ SOURCE	CBI Website 13/04/11	EC Report Graduate Employability 11/10	Dearing Report (1997)	Eurobarometer on Graduate Employability 12/10
Entrepreneuralism	✓			
Innovative approach	✓			
Creative thinking	✓			
Fresh knowledge	✓			
Challenge assumptions	✓			
Relationship building/Networking				

Higher Education Academy & CIHE: Student Employability Profiles (2006)							
Learning Skills Network: Employability Skills Explored (2008)		✓					
PWC: Being the one with the foot in the door (2010)			✓	✓			✓
Specialist Schools and Academies Trust: Applied Learning Making Learning Work							
UKCES Ambition 2020 07/05/09							
UKCES The Employability Challenge 02/09				✓			
HECSU, ACGAS: What do Graduates do? (2010)		✓					✓

APPENDIX

INDEX

Index